PHARMACEUTICAL ANALYSIS

FOR 1ST YEAR B. PHARM

DR.L. SURENDRA BABU, DR. S.PRASANTHI, DR. N. USHA RANI

Made with ♥ on the Notion Press Platform
www.notionpress.com

Contents

Preface

Pharmaceutical analysis is a critical aspect of the pharmaceutical industry, ensuring the quality, safety, and efficacy of drugs and pharmaceutical products. It encompasses a wide range of techniques and applications that are essential for pharmaceutical scientists, researchers, and professionals in the field. This book, "Pharmaceutical Analysis: Techniques and Applications," provides a comprehensive overview of the various analytical techniques used in pharmaceutical analysis and their practical applications.

Authored by Dr. L. Surendra Babu, Dr. S. Prasanthi, and Dr. N. Usha Rani, this book is a culmination of their extensive experience and expertise in the field of pharmaceutical analysis. It aims to serve as a comprehensive reference for students, researchers, and professionals in the pharmaceutical industry.

The book is organized into several chapters, each focusing on a specific analytical technique or application. Starting with an introduction to pharmaceutical analysis and its importance, the book covers a wide range of topics including chromatographic techniques, spectroscopic methods, electrochemical analysis, and more. Each chapter provides a detailed explanation of the principles behind the technique, followed by its practical applications in pharmaceutical analysis.

One of the key highlights of this book is its emphasis on practical applications. Each technique is explained in a clear and concise manner, with practical examples and case studies to illustrate its use in pharmaceutical analysis. Additionally, the book includes discussions on recent advancements in the field, such as the use of nanotechnology and molecular imaging in pharmaceutical analysis.

We hope that this book will serve as a valuable resource for students, researchers, and professionals in the field of pharmaceutical analysis. It is our sincere belief that a thorough understanding of the analytical techniques and their applications presented in this book will enhance the quality and efficiency of pharmaceutical analysis, ultimately leading to the development of safer and more effective pharmaceutical products.

Dr. L. Surendra Babu

Dr. S. Prasanthi

Dr. N. Usha Rani

Pharmaceutical Analysis: For 1st Year B.pharm

BY
Dr. LAGU SURENDRA BABU M.Pharm, Ph.D.,
Assistant Professor,
Department of Pharmaceutical Chemistry
Adikavi Nannaya University College of Pharmaceutical Sciences,
AKNU- TPG Campus
Tadepalligudem -534101
Andhra Pradesh, India.
Dr. SARAKULA PRASANTHI M.Sc., Ph.D. ,
Assistant Professor
Department of Chemistry
Adikavi Nannaya University
AKNU- TPG Campus
Tadepalligudem -534101
Andhra Pradesh, India.
Dr. NAMMI USHA RANI M. Pharm, Ph.D.,
Professor
Department of Pharmaceutical Analysis
Maharajah's College of Pharmacy,
Vizianagaram-535002
Andhra Pradesh, India.

Published by Notion Press

Notion Press, Inc.
800, West EI Camino Real #180,
California USA 94040

Notion Press Media Pvt Ltd,
#7, Red Cross Road,
Egmore, Chennai, Tamil Nadu 600008

Email ID: publish@notionpress.com

Phone Number: +91 44 46315631

CHAPTER I

Introduction to Pharmaceutical Analysis

1.1 Definition and Scope of Pharmaceutical Analysis

1.1.1 Importance in the Pharmaceutical Industry

Pharmaceutical analysis is a critical component in the **pharmaceutical industry**, serving as the backbone for ensuring the **quality, safety,** and **efficacy** of medicinal products. It involves the application of various analytical techniques and methodologies to identify the **chemical composition** of pharmaceutical substances, determine their **purity,** and quantify their **active ingredients.** The primary goal is to ensure that pharmaceutical products meet stringent **regulatory standards** and are safe for consumption.

The pharmaceutical industry is heavily regulated by national and international bodies, such as the **U.S. Food and Drug Administration (FDA),** the **European Medicines Agency (EMA),** and the **Indian Pharmacopoeia Commission (IPC).** These organizations set rigorous guidelines for the **manufacture, quality control,** and **distribution** of pharmaceutical products. **Pharmaceutical analysis** plays a pivotal role in complying with these regulations, as it provides the necessary data to demonstrate that products are consistent with the **specifications** defined in regulatory submissions.

One of the primary reasons pharmaceutical analysis is indispensable is the necessity to ensure the **consistency** and **reproducibility** of medicinal products. Each batch of a pharmaceutical product must meet the same **quality standards** to ensure that patients receive the same **therapeutic benefits** every time they use the medication. This consistency is achieved through thorough **analytical testing** at various stages of the **drug development process**, including raw material testing, in-process testing, and final product testing.

Quality control is an essential aspect of pharmaceutical analysis. It involves the routine inspection of pharmaceutical products to ensure they meet predefined standards. Analytical methods are used to test for **contaminants, impurities,** and **degradation products** that might have arisen during the manufacturing process. For instance, **chromatographic techniques** such as **High-Performance Liquid Chromatography (HPLC)** and **Gas Chromatography (GC)** are commonly employed to separate and identify impurities. These techniques offer high **sensitivity** and **accuracy**, making them ideal for detecting even trace amounts of contaminants.

Pharmaceutical analysis also plays a crucial role in the development of **new drugs**. During the drug development process, extensive testing is conducted to determine the **pharmacokinetic** and **pharmacodynamic** properties of new compounds. Analytical techniques are used to study the **absorption, distribution, metabolism,** and **excretion** (ADME) of drugs in the body. This information is vital for understanding the **drug's behavior** in vivo and for designing appropriate **dosage forms.**

Moreover, pharmaceutical analysis is integral to the formulation of **dosage forms.** Different dosage forms, such as **tablets, capsules, injectables,** and **topical preparations,** require specific analytical methods to ensure uniformity and stability. For example, **dissolution testing** is a critical analytical method for oral dosage forms, as it helps to predict how the drug will dissolve and be absorbed in the gastrointestinal tract. This testing ensures that the drug will release its active ingredients at the desired rate and extent.

In the realm of **regulatory compliance,** pharmaceutical analysis provides the data necessary for the approval of new drugs and the maintenance of existing drug licenses. Regulatory bodies require comprehensive analytical data to approve a new drug for market release. This data includes information on the drug's **identity, strength, quality, purity,** and **stability.** Stability testing, in particular, is crucial as it determines the shelf life of a drug product. It involves subjecting the drug to various **environmental conditions** (temperature, humidity, light) and analyzing its stability over time.

The advent of **biotechnology** has further expanded the scope of pharmaceutical analysis. Biopharmaceuticals, such as **monoclonal antibodies, vaccines,** and **gene therapies,** require sophisticated analytical techniques for their characterization. **Bioanalytical methods,** such as **mass spectrometry** and **nuclear magnetic resonance (NMR),** are employed to analyze complex biological molecules. These techniques provide detailed information on the **molecular structure, purity,** and **biological activity** of biopharmaceuticals.

Pharmaceutical analysis is also crucial in the field of **pharmacovigilance**, which involves monitoring the **safety** of pharmaceutical products after they have been released to the market. Analytical methods are used to investigate **adverse drug reactions** (ADRs) and to identify potential **safety issues** with marketed drugs. This ongoing surveillance helps to ensure that any **risks** associated with pharmaceutical products are promptly identified and mitigated.

In addition to ensuring the quality and safety of pharmaceutical products, pharmaceutical analysis contributes to **cost efficiency** in the pharmaceutical industry. By identifying impurities and optimizing manufacturing processes, analytical methods help to reduce **waste** and improve **yield**. This, in turn, lowers production costs and ensures that high-quality medicines are available to patients at affordable prices.

Furthermore, the field of pharmaceutical analysis is constantly evolving with advancements in technology. The development of new analytical instruments and techniques, such as **high-resolution mass spectrometry** and **advanced chromatographic methods**, continues to enhance the accuracy, sensitivity, and speed of pharmaceutical analysis. These advancements enable more precise characterization of pharmaceutical substances and more effective quality control.

The educational aspect of pharmaceutical analysis is also noteworthy. It forms a fundamental part of the curriculum for pharmacy students, equipping them with the necessary skills and knowledge to perform analytical tasks in their professional careers. Understanding the principles and applications of various analytical techniques is crucial for future pharmacists, analysts, and researchers in the pharmaceutical industry.

Pharmaceutical analysis is a cornerstone of the pharmaceutical industry, underpinning every aspect of drug development, manufacturing, and quality control. Its importance cannot be overstated, as it ensures that pharmaceutical products are safe, effective, and of high quality. Through rigorous analytical testing and adherence to regulatory standards, pharmaceutical analysis protects public health and fosters trust in the medications that people rely on for their well-being. The continuous advancement in analytical techniques and technologies promises to further enhance the capabilities and scope of pharmaceutical analysis in the future.

1.1.2 Overview of Analytical Techniques

Analytical techniques are essential tools in the **pharmaceutical industry**, used to determine the **composition, purity,** and **potency** of drug substances and products. These techniques are varied and multifaceted, allowing for the comprehensive analysis of pharmaceutical compounds through both qualitative and quantitative methods. The development and implementation of these techniques are crucial for ensuring that pharmaceutical products meet strict **regulatory standards** and are safe and effective for patient use. In this section, we will explore a range of analytical techniques, delving into their principles, methodologies, and applications in pharmaceutical analysis.

1. Chromatography Chromatography is a widely used analytical technique for separating, identifying, and quantifying components in a mixture. It involves passing a mixture dissolved in a "mobile phase" through a "stationary phase," which separates the mixture into its individual components based on their interactions with the stationary phase. The main types of chromatography used in pharmaceutical analysis are:

1.1 High-Performance Liquid Chromatography (HPLC) HPLC is one of the most common forms of chromatography in the pharmaceutical industry. It involves pumping a liquid sample through a column packed with a solid adsorbent material. The different components of the sample move through the column at different rates, allowing them to be separated and analyzed. HPLC is highly versatile and can be used for both qualitative and quantitative analysis. It is particularly useful for the analysis of complex mixtures, stability testing, and the determination of drug purity.

1.2 Gas Chromatography (GC) GC is used to separate and analyze compounds that can be vaporized without decomposition. It involves passing a gaseous sample through a column containing a liquid stationary phase. The components of the sample separate based on their boiling points and interactions with the stationary phase. GC is especially useful for the analysis of volatile compounds, such as residual solvents in pharmaceutical products.

1.3 Thin Layer Chromatography (TLC) TLC is a simple, quick, and cost-effective chromatographic technique. It involves applying a small amount of sample to a plate coated with a thin layer of adsorbent material (usually silica gel). The plate is then placed in a solvent, which travels up the plate by capillary action, separating the components of the sample. TLC is commonly used for qualitative analysis, such as identifying compounds and checking the purity of substances.

1.4 Size Exclusion Chromatography (SEC) SEC, also known as gel filtration chromatography, separates molecules based on their size. It involves passing a sample through a column packed with porous beads. Smaller molecules enter the pores and take longer to elute, while larger molecules pass through more quickly. SEC is particularly useful for the analysis of proteins and polymers in pharmaceutical formulations.

2. Spectroscopy Spectroscopy involves the interaction of light with matter to produce spectra that can be used to identify and quantify substances. Different types of spectroscopy are used in pharmaceutical analysis, each providing unique information about the sample being studied.

2.1 Ultraviolet-Visible (UV-Vis) Spectroscopy UV-Vis spectroscopy measures the absorption of ultraviolet or visible light by a substance. It is commonly used to determine the concentration of a compound in a solution. The technique is based on the principle that molecules absorb light at specific wavelengths, producing a characteristic absorption spectrum. UV-Vis spectroscopy is widely used in the pharmaceutical industry for the analysis of drug formulations and the determination of drug stability.

2.2 Infrared (IR) Spectroscopy IR spectroscopy measures the absorption of infrared light by a substance, providing information about its molecular structure. Different functional groups in a molecule absorb IR light at specific wavelengths, producing a characteristic absorption spectrum. IR spectroscopy is used to identify unknown compounds, determine the purity of substances, and study the interactions between drugs and excipients.

2.3 Nuclear Magnetic Resonance (NMR) Spectroscopy NMR spectroscopy involves the interaction of nuclear spins with an external magnetic field, producing spectra that provide detailed information about the molecular structure and dynamics of a compound. NMR spectroscopy is particularly useful for the identification and structural elucidation of organic compounds. It is also used to study the conformation and interactions of biomolecules, such as proteins and nucleic acids.

2.4 Mass Spectrometry (MS) MS measures the mass-to-charge ratio of ions, providing information about the molecular weight and structure of a compound. The technique involves ionizing the sample, separating the ions based on their mass-to-charge ratio, and detecting them to produce a mass spectrum. MS is highly sensitive and can be used for both qualitative and quantitative analysis. It is often coupled with other techniques, such as chromatography, to provide more comprehensive analysis.

3. Titrimetry Titrimetry involves the quantitative determination of a substance by reacting it with a known concentration of a reagent (titrant). The endpoint of the titration is detected using an indicator or an instrument.

3.1 Acid-Base Titration Acid-base titration involves the reaction of an acid with a base to determine the concentration of one of the reactants. Indicators or pH meters are used to detect the endpoint. This technique is widely used in pharmaceutical analysis to determine the potency of acidic or basic drugs and excipients.

3.2 Redox Titration Redox titration involves the transfer of electrons between the analyte and the titrant. The endpoint is detected using redox indicators or potentiometric methods. Redox titrations are used to analyze compounds that undergo oxidation or reduction reactions, such as antioxidants and oxidizing agents.

3.3 Complexometric Titration Complexometric titration involves the formation of a complex between the analyte and the titrant. The endpoint is detected using metal ion indicators or instrumental methods. This technique is particularly useful for the determination of metal ions in pharmaceutical formulations.

3.4 Precipitation Titration Precipitation titration involves the formation of an insoluble precipitate during the reaction between the analyte and the titrant. The endpoint is detected by observing the formation of the precipitate or using indicators. Precipitation titrations are used to analyze compounds that form insoluble salts, such as halides.

4. Electrochemical Analysis Electrochemical analysis involves the measurement of electrical properties (such as voltage, current, or charge) to determine the concentration of analytes. This technique is highly sensitive and can be used for the analysis of both organic and inorganic compounds.

4.1 Potentiometry Potentiometry measures the voltage of an electrochemical cell to determine the concentration of an analyte. The technique involves using a reference electrode and an indicator electrode. Potentiometric methods are used for the determination of pH, ion concentration, and redox potential in pharmaceutical analysis.

4.2 Conductometry Conductometry measures the electrical conductivity of a solution to determine the concentration of an analyte. The technique involves passing an electric current through the solution and measuring the resulting conductivity. Conductometric methods are used for the analysis of electrolytes and the determination of the purity of water and other solvents.

4.3 Polarography Polarography measures the current that flows in an electrochemical cell under a varying voltage to determine the concentration of an analyte. The technique involves using a dropping mercury electrode or a rotating platinum electrode. Polarographic methods are used for the analysis of metal ions and organic compounds in pharmaceutical formulations.

5. Thermal Analysis Thermal analysis involves the measurement of changes in physical or chemical properties of a substance as a function of temperature. This technique provides information about the thermal stability, composition, and purity of pharmaceutical compounds.

5.1 Differential Scanning Calorimetry (DSC) DSC measures the heat flow associated with phase transitions and chemical reactions as a function of temperature. This technique is used to study the thermal stability, melting point, and crystallinity of pharmaceutical compounds.

5.2 Thermogravimetric Analysis (TGA) TGA measures the change in mass of a substance as a function of temperature. This technique is used to study the thermal stability, decomposition, and moisture content of pharmaceutical compounds.

5.3 Differential Thermal Analysis (DTA) DTA measures the temperature difference between a sample and a reference as a function of temperature. This technique is used to study phase transitions and chemical reactions in pharmaceutical compounds.

6. Microscopy Microscopy involves the use of microscopes to visualize and analyze the physical structure of pharmaceutical compounds. Different types of microscopy provide different levels of detail and information.

6.1 Optical Microscopy Optical microscopy uses visible light to magnify and visualize small structures. This technique is used to study the morphology, particle size, and distribution of pharmaceutical compounds.

6.2 Scanning Electron Microscopy (SEM) SEM uses a focused beam of electrons to produce high-resolution images of the surface of a sample. This technique is used to study the surface morphology and composition of pharmaceutical compounds.

6.3 Transmission Electron Microscopy (TEM) TEM uses a beam of electrons transmitted through a sample to produce high-resolution images of its internal structure. This technique is used to study the internal morphology and composition of pharmaceutical compounds.

7. Spectrophotometry Spectrophotometry involves measuring the amount of light absorbed or transmitted by a substance at different wavelengths. This technique provides information about the concentration and chemical structure of the substance.

7.1 UV-Visible Spectrophotometry UV-Visible spectrophotometry measures the absorption of ultraviolet and visible light by a substance. This technique is used to determine the concentration and purity of pharmaceutical compounds.

7.2 Infrared Spectrophotometry Infrared spectrophotometry measures the absorption of infrared light by a substance. This technique is used to identify functional groups and study the molecular structure of pharmaceutical compounds.

7.3 Fluorescence Spectrophotometry Fluorescence spectrophotometry measures the emission of light by a substance after it has absorbed light. This technique is used to determine the concentration and study the interactions of fluorescent compounds in pharmaceutical formulations.

8. X-Ray Analysis X-Ray analysis involves the use of X-rays to study the crystal structure and composition of pharmaceutical compounds.

8.1 X-Ray Diffraction (XRD) XRD measures the diffraction of X-rays by the crystal lattice of a substance. This technique is used to determine the crystal structure, polymorphism, and purity of pharmaceutical compounds.

8.2 X-Ray Fluorescence (XRF) XRF measures the emission of secondary X-rays from a substance after it has been excited by primary X-rays. This technique is used to determine the elemental composition and purity of pharmaceutical compounds.

9. Nuclear Magnetic Resonance (NMR) Spectroscopy NMR spectroscopy involves the interaction of nuclear spins with an external magnetic field to produce spectra that provide detailed information about the molecular structure and dynamics of a compound.

9.1 Proton NMR (1H NMR) 1H NMR measures the interaction of hydrogen nuclei with an external magnetic field. This technique is used to determine the structure and purity of organic compounds in pharmaceutical formulations.

9.2 Carbon-13 NMR (13C NMR) 13C NMR measures the interaction of carbon-13 nuclei with an external magnetic field. This technique is used to determine the structure and composition of organic compounds in pharmaceutical formulations.

10. Mass Spectrometry (MS) MS measures the mass-to-charge ratio of ions to provide information about the molecular weight and structure of a compound. The technique involves ionizing the sample, separating the ions based on their mass-to-charge ratio, and detecting them to produce a mass spectrum.

10.1 Electron Ionization (EI) EI involves ionizing a sample by bombarding it with electrons. This technique is used to determine the molecular weight and fragmentation pattern of organic compounds in pharmaceutical formulations.

10.2 Electrospray Ionization (ESI) ESI involves ionizing a sample by applying a high voltage to a liquid sample. This technique is used to analyze large biomolecules, such as proteins and nucleic acids, in pharmaceutical formulations.

10.3 Matrix-Assisted Laser Desorption/Ionization (MALDI) MALDI involves ionizing a sample by irradiating it with a laser. This technique is used to analyze large biomolecules and polymers in pharmaceutical formulations.

The diverse range of **analytical techniques** available for **pharmaceutical analysis** enables the comprehensive examination of drug substances and products. Each technique offers unique insights into the composition, structure, and purity of pharmaceuticals, ensuring that they meet the highest standards of quality and safety. Through the meticulous application of these techniques, the **pharmaceutical industry** can continue to develop and produce effective medications that improve patient outcomes and advance public health.

1.2 Methods of Expressing Concentration

Concentration is a crucial parameter in pharmaceutical analysis, as it determines the amount of active pharmaceutical ingredient (API) or other components present in a formulation. Various methods are used to express concentration, each providing different insights into the composition of a pharmaceutical product. In this section, we will explore the different methods of expressing concentration and their significance in pharmaceutical analysis.

1. Mass Percentage (% w/w)

Mass percentage (% w/w) is a common method of expressing concentration, particularly for solid formulations. It is defined as the mass of the solute (API or other components) divided by the total mass of the solution, multiplied by 100. For example, a 5% w/w solution of a drug in a tablet means that 5 grams of the drug are present in 100 grams of the tablet.

2. Volume Percentage (% v/v)

Volume percentage (% v/v) is used to express the concentration of liquid formulations. It is defined as the volume of the solute (API or other components) divided by the total volume of the solution, multiplied by 100. For example, a 10% v/v solution of alcohol means that 10 milliliters of alcohol are present in 100 milliliters of the solution.

3. Parts per Million (ppm)

Parts per million (ppm) is a method of expressing very low concentrations of a substance in a solution. It is defined as the mass of the solute (in milligrams) divided by the total mass of the solution (in kilograms), multiplied by 10^6. For example, a water sample with 1 ppm of a contaminant means that there is 1 milligram of the contaminant present in 1 kilogram of water.

4. Molarity (M)

Molarity (M) is a measure of concentration that relates the number of moles of solute to the volume of the solution in liters. It is defined as the number of moles of solute divided by the volume of the solution in liters. For example, a 0.1 M solution of a drug means that there is 0.1 moles of the drug present in 1 liter of the solution.

5. Molality (m)

Molality (m) is similar to molarity, but it relates the number of moles of solute to the mass of the solvent in kilograms. It is defined as the number of moles of solute divided by the mass of the solvent in kilograms. Molality is particularly useful in situations where the volume of the solution may change, such as in reactions involving temperature changes.

6. Normality (N)

Normality (N) is a measure of concentration that takes into account the equivalents of a solute rather than just the moles. It is defined as the number of equivalents of solute divided by the volume of the solution in liters. Normality is often used in acid-base titrations, where the reaction involves the transfer of protons (H+ ions).

7. Percentage (%) Solutions

Percentage solutions are expressed as the number of grams of solute present in 100 milliliters of the solution. For example, a 10% solution of a drug means that there are 10 grams of the drug present in 100 milliliters of the solution.

8. Parts per Thousand (ppt)

Parts per thousand (ppt) is similar to ppm but is used for expressing concentrations that are higher than ppm but lower than percent. It is defined as the mass of the solute (in grams) divided by the total mass of the solution (in kilograms), multiplied by 1000. For example, a solution with a concentration of 2 ppt means that there are 2 grams of the solute present in 1000 grams of the solution.

The choice of method for expressing concentration in pharmaceutical analysis depends on the nature of the formulation, the concentration range of the solute, and the specific requirements of the analysis. Each method offers unique advantages and is used to provide different insights into the composition of pharmaceutical products. Understanding these methods is essential for accurate and precise analysis in the pharmaceutical industry.

Unit	Symbol	Definition
Molarity	M	Moles of solute per liter of solution
Normality	N	Equivalents of solute per liter of solution
Molality	m	Moles of solute per kilogram of solvent
Percent (% w/v)	% w/v	Grams of solute per 100 milliliters of solution
Percent (% w/w)	% w/w	Grams of solute per 100 grams of solution
Parts per million	ppm	Milligrams of solute per liter of solution
Parts per billion	ppb	Micrograms of solute per liter of solution

Table 1: Common Units of Concentration

1.2.1 Molarity

Molarity (M) is a widely used method for expressing the concentration of a solute in a solution. It is defined as the number of moles of solute dissolved in one liter of solution. Molarity is represented by the formula:

M=<u>Number of moles of solute</u>

Volume of solution in liters

For example, if you dissolve 0.5 moles of sodium chloride (NaCl) in enough water to make 1 liter of solution, the molarity of the solution would be 0.5 M.

Significance in Pharmaceutical Analysis

Molarity is particularly important in pharmaceutical analysis for several reasons:

1. **Quantitative Analysis:** Molarity allows for the precise determination of the concentration of a solute in a solution. This is crucial in pharmaceutical analysis, where the accurate measurement of drug concentrations is essential for ensuring the safety and efficacy of medications.
2. **Reaction Stoichiometry:** Molarity is used to calculate the stoichiometry of reactions involving solutions. This is important in pharmaceutical analysis for determining the purity of drug substances and the composition of pharmaceutical formulations.
3. **Standardization of Solutions:** Molarity is used to standardize solutions, such as acids and bases, which are commonly used in pharmaceutical analysis for titrations and other analytical techniques.
4. **Dilution Calculations:** Molarity is used to calculate the concentration of a solution after it has been diluted. This is important in pharmaceutical analysis for preparing solutions with specific concentrations for use in analytical procedures.

Molarity is a fundamental concept in pharmaceutical analysis, providing a quantitative measure of the concentration of a solute in a solution. Understanding molarity is essential for conducting accurate and precise analyses in the pharmaceutical industry, ensuring the quality and safety of pharmaceutical products.

1.2.2 Normality

Normality (N) is a measure of concentration that takes into account the equivalents of a solute rather than just the moles. It is defined as the number of equivalents of solute per liter of solution. Normality is represented by the formula:

N=<u>Number of equivalents of solute</u>

Volume of solution in liters

where the number of equivalents is determined by the reaction stoichiometry. For example, if a reaction involves the transfer of one mole of protons (H^+ ions), the normality of the solution containing the acid would be equal to its molarity.

Significance in Pharmaceutical Analysis

Normality is particularly important in pharmaceutical analysis for several reasons:

1. **Acid-Base Titrations:** Normality is commonly used in acid-base titrations, where the reaction involves the transfer of protons (H^+ ions). In such titrations, the normality of the acid or base is used to calculate the equivalent volume required to reach the equivalence point.

2. **Redox Titrations:** Normality is also used in redox titrations, where the reaction involves the transfer of electrons. In these titrations, the normality of the oxidizing or reducing agent is used to calculate the equivalent volume required to reach the equivalence point.

3. **Complexometric Titrations:** Normality is used in complexometric titrations, where the reaction involves the formation of a complex between the analyte and the titrant. The normality of the titrant is used to calculate the concentration of the analyte.

4. **Precipitation Titrations:** Normality is used in precipitation titrations, where the reaction involves the formation of an insoluble precipitate. The normality of the titrant is used to calculate the concentration of the analyte.

Normality is an important concept in pharmaceutical analysis, particularly in titrimetric methods where it is used to calculate the equivalent volume of a titrant required to react with a given amount of analyte. Understanding normality is essential for conducting accurate and precise titrations in the pharmaceutical industry, ensuring the quality and safety of pharmaceutical products.

1.2.3 Other Concentration Units

In addition to molarity and normality, there are several other concentration units commonly used in pharmaceutical analysis. These units are used to express the concentration of a solute in a solution in different ways, depending on the specific requirements of the analysis. Some of the other concentration units include:

1. Molality (m) Molality is similar to molarity, but it relates the number of moles of solute to the mass of the solvent in kilograms. It is defined as the number of moles of solute divided by the mass of the solvent in kilograms. Molality is represented by the formula: m=Number of moles of solute Mass of solvent in

Number of moles of solute Molality is particularly useful in situations where the volume of the solution may change, such as in reactions involving temperature changes.

2. Mass Percentage (% w/w) Mass percentage is a method of expressing concentration as the mass of the solute (API or other components) divided by the total mass of the solution, multiplied by 100. Mass percentage is represented by the formula:

%w/w= <u>Mass of solute</u> X 100

Total mass of solution

Mass percentage is commonly used for solid formulations.

3. Volume Percentage (% v/v) Volume percentage is used to express the concentration of liquid formulations. It is defined as the volume of the solute (API or other components) divided by the total volume of the solution, multiplied by 100. Volume percentage is represented by the formula: %v/v=<u>Volume of solute</u> X 100

Total volume of solution

4. Parts per Million (ppm) Parts per million is a method of expressing very low concentrations of a substance in a solution. It is defined as the mass of the solute (in milligrams) divided by the total mass of the solution (in kilograms), multiplied by 10^6.

Parts per million is represented by the formula:

ppm=<u>Mass of solute in mg </u>$\times 10^6$

Total mass of solution in kg

5. Parts per Thousand (ppt) Parts per thousand is similar to ppm but is used for expressing concentrations that are higher than ppm but lower than percent. It is defined as the mass of the solute (in grams) divided by the total mass of the solution (in kilograms), multiplied by 1000.

Parts per thousand is represented by the formula:

ppt=<u>Mass of solute in </u>$\times 1000$

Total mass of solution in kg

These concentration units provide flexibility in expressing the concentration of a solute in a solution, allowing for precise and accurate analysis in pharmaceutical formulations. Understanding these units is essential for conducting analytical procedures in the pharmaceutical industry, ensuring the quality and safety of pharmaceutical products.

1.3 Standards in Analytical Chemistry

Standards play a crucial role in analytical chemistry, providing reference points for the accurate and precise measurement of substances. They are used to calibrate instruments, validate analytical methods, and ensure the accuracy of analytical results. In pharmaceutical analysis, standards are particularly important due to the strict quality and safety requirements of pharmaceutical products. This section will discuss the different types of standards used in analytical chemistry, starting with primary standards.

1.3.1 Primary Standards

Introduction

Primary standards are highly pure compounds that are used to establish the exact concentration of solutions used in analytical procedures. These compounds have known and well-defined properties, making them ideal for calibrating instruments and validating analytical methods. Primary standards are essential for ensuring the accuracy and reliability of analytical measurements in pharmaceutical analysis.

Preparation of Primary Standards

The preparation of primary standards involves several steps to ensure their purity and accuracy:

1. **Selection of Compound:** A compound is selected based on its purity, stability, and availability. Common primary standards include potassium hydrogen phthalate (KHP) for acid-base titrations and potassium dichromate for redox titrations.
2. **Purification:** The selected compound is purified to remove any impurities that could affect its concentration. This may involve recrystallization, sublimation, or other purification techniques.
3. **Determination of Exact Mass:** The exact mass of the compound is determined using a balance calibrated with reference weights. This ensures that the correct amount of compound is used in the preparation of the standard solution.
4. **Dissolution:** The purified compound is dissolved in a suitable solvent to prepare a standard solution of known concentration. The concentration is determined by gravimetric or volumetric analysis.
5. **Standardization:** The standard solution is then titrated against a primary standard of known concentration to determine its exact concentration. This process is repeated several times to ensure accuracy.

Use of Primary Standards

Primary standards are used in various analytical procedures in pharmaceutical analysis:

1. **Calibration of Instruments:** Primary standards are used to calibrate instruments such as spectrophotometers, chromatographs, and pH meters to ensure accurate readings.
2. **Validation of Analytical Methods:** Primary standards are used to validate analytical methods to ensure their accuracy, precision, and reliability.
3. **Quality Control:** Primary standards are used in quality control to monitor the performance of analytical procedures and ensure the consistency of results.

In conclusion, primary standards are essential for ensuring the accuracy and reliability of analytical measurements in pharmaceutical analysis. Their use is critical for maintaining the quality and safety of pharmaceutical products and for ensuring compliance with regulatory standards.

1.3.1 Primary Standards

Introduction

Primary standards are essential in analytical chemistry as they serve as reference materials for the accurate determination of the concentration of solutions. These standards are highly pure compounds with known properties, making them ideal for calibrating instruments and validating analytical methods. In pharmaceutical analysis, primary standards play a crucial role in ensuring the accuracy and reliability of analytical measurements, which is critical for maintaining the quality and safety of pharmaceutical products.

Preparation of Primary Standards

The preparation of primary standards involves several important steps to ensure their purity and accuracy. For example, in the case of potassium hydrogen phthalate (KHP), a common primary standard used in acid-base titrations, the compound is first purified through recrystallization to remove impurities. The exact mass of the purified compound is then determined using a calibrated balance, and it is dissolved in a suitable solvent to prepare a standard solution of known concentration. This solution is then titrated against a standard solution of a primary standard, such as sodium hydroxide, to determine its exact concentration.

Example: Preparation of KHP Primary Standard

To prepare a standard solution of KHP, 2.204 g of KHP is dissolved in distilled water and diluted to 250.0 mL in a volumetric flask. This solution is then titrated against a standard solution of sodium hydroxide (NaOH) of known concentration to determine the exact concentration of the KHP solution. The reaction between KHP and NaOH is:

$$KHC_8H_4O_4 + NaOH \rightarrow NaKC_8H_4O_4 + H_2O$$

The exact concentration of the NaOH solution is known, so by measuring the volume of NaOH required to titrate the KHP solution, the concentration of the KHP solution can be calculated.

Use of Primary Standards

Primary standards are used in various analytical procedures in pharmaceutical analysis, including:

- **Calibration of Instruments:** Primary standards are used to calibrate instruments such as spectrophotometers, chromatographs, and pH meters to ensure accurate readings.
- **Validation of Analytical Methods:** Primary standards are used to validate analytical methods to ensure their accuracy, precision, and reliability.
- **Quality Control:** Primary standards are used in quality control to monitor the performance of analytical procedures and ensure the consistency of results.

In conclusion, primary standards are essential for ensuring the accuracy and reliability of analytical measurements in pharmaceutical analysis. Their use is critical for maintaining the quality and safety of pharmaceutical products and for ensuring compliance with regulatory standards.

1.3.2 Secondary Standards

Secondary standards are substances that are standardized against primary standards to establish their exact concentration. These substances are used in analytical chemistry to calibrate instruments, validate analytical methods, and ensure the accuracy of measurements. Secondary standards are particularly important in pharmaceutical analysis, where precise and accurate measurements are essential for ensuring the quality and safety of pharmaceutical products.

Preparation of Secondary Standards

The preparation of secondary standards involves several steps:

1. **Selection of Primary Standard:** A primary standard, which is a highly pure compound of known concentration, is selected based on its suitability for the analytical method being used.

2. **Standardization:** The primary standard is dissolved in a suitable solvent and titrated against a standardized solution of another compound to determine its exact concentration. This process is repeated several times to ensure accuracy.
3. **Storage:** The secondary standard solution is stored in a tightly sealed container to prevent contamination or evaporation. It is also labeled with the date of preparation and the concentration of the solution.

Use of Secondary Standards

Secondary standards are used in various analytical procedures in pharmaceutical analysis:

1. **Calibration of Instruments:** Secondary standards are used to calibrate instruments such as spectrophotometers, chromatographs, and pH meters to ensure accurate readings.
2. **Validation of Analytical Methods:** Secondary standards are used to validate analytical methods to ensure their accuracy, precision, and reliability.
3. **Quality Control:** Secondary standards are used in quality control to monitor the performance of analytical procedures and ensure the consistency of results.

In conclusion, secondary standards play a crucial role in pharmaceutical analysis by ensuring the accuracy and reliability of analytical measurements. Their use is essential for maintaining the quality and safety of pharmaceutical products and for ensuring compliance with regulatory standards.

1.3.3 Preparation and Standardization of Solutions

1.3.3.1 Oxalic Acid

Preparation of Oxalic Acid Solution

Oxalic acid ($C_2H_2O_4$) is commonly used as a primary standard in analytical chemistry due to its high purity and stability. To prepare a standard solution of oxalic acid, follow these steps:

1. **Weighing of Oxalic Acid:** Accurately weigh a known mass of oxalic acid using an analytical balance. The mass should be appropriate for the desired concentration of the solution.

2. **Dissolution of Oxalic Acid:** Transfer the weighed oxalic acid to a clean, dry beaker. Add distilled water to dissolve the oxalic acid completely. Use a glass stirring rod to aid in the dissolution process.

3. **Transfer to Volumetric Flask:** Once the oxalic acid is completely dissolved, transfer the solution to a 1000 mL volumetric flask using a funnel. Rinse the beaker several times with distilled water to ensure all the oxalic acid is transferred.

4. **Dilution to Volume:** Add distilled water to the volumetric flask until the bottom of the meniscus is at the mark on the neck of the flask. Use a dropper or a wash bottle for the final volume adjustment to avoid overfilling.

5. **Mixing the Solution:** Cap the volumetric flask and invert it several times to ensure thorough mixing of the solution. This will ensure a homogenous concentration throughout the solution.

Standardization of Oxalic Acid Solution

After preparing the oxalic acid solution, it needs to be standardized against a primary standard such as potassium permanganate (KMnO4) to determine its exact concentration. Follow these steps for standardization:

1. **Preparation of Potassium Permanganate Solution:** Prepare a standard solution of potassium permanganate of known concentration. This solution will be used as the titrant in the standardization process.

2. **Titration:** Pipette a known volume of the oxalic acid solution into a conical flask. Add a few drops of sulfuric acid (H_2SO_4) as a catalyst and titrate with the potassium permanganate solution until a permanent pink color is observed.

3. **Calculation:** The volume and concentration of the potassium permanganate solution used in the titration, along with the stoichiometry of the reaction between oxalic acid and potassium permanganate, can be used to calculate the exact concentration of the oxalic acid solution.

Significance of Oxalic Acid Solution in Analytical Chemistry

Oxalic acid solution is used as a primary standard in various analytical procedures, particularly in volumetric analysis. It is used for the standardization of solutions of bases, such as sodium hydroxide (NaOH), and as a reducing agent in certain reactions. The accurate preparation and standardization of oxalic acid solution are crucial for obtaining reliable and accurate analytical results in pharmaceutical analysis.

1.3.3.2 Sodium Hydroxide

Preparation of Sodium Hydroxide Solution

Sodium hydroxide (NaOH) is a strong base commonly used in analytical chemistry. To prepare a standard solution of sodium hydroxide, follow these steps:

1. **Weighing of Sodium Hydroxide:** Accurately weigh a known mass of sodium hydroxide using an analytical balance. The mass should be appropriate for the desired concentration of the solution.
2. **Dissolution of Sodium Hydroxide:** Transfer the weighed sodium hydroxide to a clean, dry beaker. Add distilled water to dissolve the sodium hydroxide completely. Caution should be taken as this process is exothermic and generates heat.
3. **Transfer to Volumetric Flask:** Once the sodium hydroxide is completely dissolved, transfer the solution to a 1000 mL volumetric flask using a funnel. Rinse the beaker several times with distilled water to ensure all the sodium hydroxide is transferred.
4. **Dilution to Volume:** Add distilled water to the volumetric flask until the bottom of the meniscus is at the mark on the neck of the flask. Use a dropper or a wash bottle for the final volume adjustment to avoid overfilling.
5. **Mixing the Solution:** Cap the volumetric flask and invert it several times to ensure thorough mixing of the solution. This will ensure a homogenous concentration throughout the solution.

Standardization of Sodium Hydroxide Solution

After preparing the sodium hydroxide solution, it needs to be standardized against a primary standard such as potassium hydrogen phthalate (KHP) to determine its exact concentration. Follow these steps for standardization:

1. **Preparation of KHP Solution:** Prepare a standard solution of KHP of known concentration. This solution will be used as the titrant in the standardization process.
2. **Titration:** Pipette a known volume of the KHP solution into a conical flask. Add a few drops of phenolphthalein indicator and titrate with the

sodium hydroxide solution until a faint pink color that persists for at least 30 seconds is observed.

3. **Calculation:** The volume and concentration of the sodium hydroxide solution used in the titration, along with the stoichiometry of the reaction between KHP and sodium hydroxide, can be used to calculate the exact concentration of the sodium hydroxide solution.

Significance of Sodium Hydroxide Solution in Analytical Chemistry

Sodium hydroxide solution is used as a primary standard in various analytical procedures, particularly in acid-base titrations. It is also used in the preparation of standard solutions of acids and as a reagent in various analytical tests. The accurate preparation and standardization of sodium hydroxide solution are crucial for obtaining reliable and accurate analytical results in pharmaceutical analysis.

1.3.3.3 Hydrochloric Acid

Preparation of Hydrochloric Acid Solution

Hydrochloric acid (HCl) is a strong acid commonly used in analytical chemistry. To prepare a standard solution of hydrochloric acid, follow these steps:

1. **Dilution of Concentrated Hydrochloric Acid:** Since concentrated hydrochloric acid is typically around 37% HCl by mass, it needs to be diluted to the desired concentration. To prepare a 1 M solution, for example, dilute 85 mL of concentrated hydrochloric acid to 1 liter with distilled water.

2. **Transfer to Volumetric Flask:** Carefully transfer the diluted hydrochloric acid to a 1000 mL volumetric flask using a funnel. Rinse the container several times with distilled water to ensure all the acid is transferred.

3. **Dilution to Volume:** Add distilled water to the volumetric flask until the bottom of the meniscus is at the mark on the neck of the flask. Use a dropper or a wash bottle for the final volume adjustment to avoid overfilling.

4. **Mixing the Solution:** Cap the volumetric flask and invert it several times to ensure thorough mixing of the solution. This will ensure a homogenous concentration throughout the solution.

Standardization of Hydrochloric Acid Solution

After preparing the hydrochloric acid solution, it needs to be standardized against a primary standard such as sodium carbonate (Na2CO3) to determine its exact concentration. Follow these steps for standardization:

1. **Preparation of Sodium Carbonate Solution:** Prepare a standard solution of sodium carbonate of known concentration. This solution will be used as the titrant in the standardization process.
2. **Titration:** Pipette a known volume of the sodium carbonate solution into a conical flask. Add a few drops of methyl orange indicator and titrate with the hydrochloric acid solution until a color change from orange to pink is observed.
3. **Calculation:** The volume and concentration of the hydrochloric acid solution used in the titration, along with the stoichiometry of the reaction between sodium carbonate and hydrochloric acid, can be used to calculate the exact concentration of the hydrochloric acid solution.

Significance of Hydrochloric Acid Solution in Analytical Chemistry

Hydrochloric acid solution is used as a standard solution in various analytical procedures, particularly in acid-base titrations. It is also used as a reagent in various analytical tests. The accurate preparation and standardization of hydrochloric acid solution are crucial for obtaining reliable and accurate analytical results in pharmaceutical analysis.

1.3.3.4 Sodium Thiosulfate

Preparation of Sodium Thiosulfate Solution

Sodium thiosulfate ($Na_2S_2O_3$) is commonly used in analytical chemistry, particularly in iodometric titrations. To prepare a standard solution of sodium thiosulfate, follow these steps:

1. **Weighing of Sodium Thiosulfate:** Accurately weigh a known mass of sodium thiosulfate using an analytical balance. The mass should be appropriate for the desired concentration of the solution.
2. **Dissolution of Sodium Thiosulfate:** Transfer the weighed sodium thiosulfate to a clean, dry beaker. Add distilled water to dissolve the sodium thiosulfate completely.

3. **Transfer to Volumetric Flask:** Once the sodium thiosulfate is completely dissolved, transfer the solution to a 1000 mL volumetric flask using a funnel. Rinse the beaker several times with distilled water to ensure all the sodium thiosulfate is transferred.

4. **Dilution to Volume:** Add distilled water to the volumetric flask until the bottom of the meniscus is at the mark on the neck of the flask. Use a dropper or a wash bottle for the final volume adjustment to avoid overfilling.

5. **Mixing the Solution:** Cap the volumetric flask and invert it several times to ensure thorough mixing of the solution. This will ensure a homogenous concentration throughout the solution.

Standardization of Sodium Thiosulfate Solution

After preparing the sodium thiosulfate solution, it needs to be standardized against a primary standard such as potassium iodate (KIO3) to determine its exact concentration. Follow these steps for standardization:

1. **Preparation of Potassium Iodate Solution:** Prepare a standard solution of potassium iodate of known concentration. This solution will be used as the titrant in the standardization process.

2. **Titration:** Pipette a known volume of the potassium iodate solution into a conical flask. Add a few drops of starch indicator and titrate with the sodium thiosulfate solution until the blue-black color of the starch-iodine complex disappears.

3. **Calculation:** The volume and concentration of the sodium thiosulfate solution used in the titration, along with the stoichiometry of the reaction between potassium iodate and sodium thiosulfate, can be used to calculate the exact concentration of the sodium thiosulfate solution.

Significance of Sodium Thiosulfate Solution in Analytical Chemistry

Sodium thiosulfate solution is used as a standard solution in iodometric titrations, particularly for the determination of substances that react with iodine. It is also used as a reducing agent in various analytical procedures. The accurate preparation and standardization of sodium thiosulfate solution are crucial for obtaining reliable and accurate analytical results in pharmaceutical analysis.

1.3.3.5 Sulphuric Acid

Preparation of Sulphuric Acid Solution

Sulphuric acid (H_2SO_4) is a strong acid commonly used in analytical chemistry. To prepare a standard solution of sulphuric acid, follow these steps:

1. **Dilution of Concentrated Sulphuric Acid:** Since concentrated sulphuric acid is typically around 95-98% H_2SO_4, it needs to be diluted to the desired concentration. To prepare a 1 M solution, for example, dilute 27.5 mL of concentrated sulphuric acid to 1 liter with distilled water.
2. **Transfer to Volumetric Flask:** Carefully transfer the diluted sulphuric acid to a 1000 mL volumetric flask using a funnel. Rinse the container several times with distilled water to ensure all the acid is transferred.
3. **Dilution to Volume:** Add distilled water to the volumetric flask until the bottom of the meniscus is at the mark on the neck of the flask. Use a dropper or a wash bottle for the final volume adjustment to avoid overfilling.
4. **Mixing the Solution:** Cap the volumetric flask and invert it several times to ensure thorough mixing of the solution. This will ensure a homogenous concentration throughout the solution.

Standardization of Sulphuric Acid Solution

After preparing the sulphuric acid solution, it needs to be standardized against a primary standard such as sodium carbonate (Na_2CO_3) to determine its exact concentration. Follow these steps for standardization:

1. **Preparation of Sodium Carbonate Solution:** Prepare a standard solution of sodium carbonate of known concentration. This solution will be used as the titrant in the standardization process.
2. **Titration:** Pipette a known volume of the sodium carbonate solution into a conical flask. Add a few drops of methyl orange indicator and titrate with the sulphuric acid solution until a color change from yellow to orange is observed.
3. **Calculation:** The volume and concentration of the sulphuric acid solution used in the titration, along with the stoichiometry of the reaction between sodium carbonate and sulphuric acid, can be used to calculate the exact concentration of the sulphuric acid solution.

Significance of Sulphuric Acid Solution in Analytical Chemistry

Sulphuric acid solution is used as a standard solution in various analytical procedures, particularly in acid-base titrations. It is also used as a dehydrating agent and in the preparation of standard solutions of acids. The accurate preparation and standardization of sulphuric acid solution are crucial for obtaining reliable and accurate analytical results in pharmaceutical analysis.

1.3.3.6 Potassium Permanganate

Preparation of Potassium Permanganate Solution

Potassium permanganate (KMnO4) is a strong oxidizing agent commonly used in analytical chemistry. To prepare a standard solution of potassium permanganate, follow these steps:

1. **Weighing of Potassium Permanganate:** Accurately weigh a known mass of potassium permanganate using an analytical balance. The mass should be appropriate for the desired concentration of the solution.
2. **Dissolution of Potassium Permanganate:** Transfer the weighed potassium permanganate to a clean, dry beaker. Add distilled water to dissolve the potassium permanganate completely.
3. **Transfer to Volumetric Flask:** Once the potassium permanganate is completely dissolved, transfer the solution to a 1000 mL volumetric flask using a funnel. Rinse the beaker several times with distilled water to ensure all the potassium permanganate is transferred.
4. **Dilution to Volume:** Add distilled water to the volumetric flask until the bottom of the meniscus is at the mark on the neck of the flask. Use a dropper or a wash bottle for the final volume adjustment to avoid overfilling.
5. **Mixing the Solution:** Cap the volumetric flask and invert it several times to ensure thorough mixing of the solution. This will ensure a homogenous concentration throughout the solution.

Standardization of Potassium Permanganate Solution

After preparing the potassium permanganate solution, it needs to be standardized against a primary standard such as oxalic acid $(C_2H_2O_4)$ to determine its exact concentration. Follow these steps for standardization:

1. **Preparation of Oxalic Acid Solution:** Prepare a standard solution of oxalic acid of known concentration. This solution will be used as the titrant in the standardization process.

2. **Titration:** Pipette a known volume of the oxalic acid solution into a conical flask. Add a few drops of sulfuric acid (H_2SO_4) as a catalyst and titrate with the potassium permanganate solution until a permanent pink color is observed.

3. **Calculation:** The volume and concentration of the potassium permanganate solution used in the titration, along with the stoichiometry of the reaction between oxalic acid and potassium permanganate, can be used to calculate the exact concentration of the potassium permanganate solution.

Significance of Potassium Permanganate Solution in Analytical Chemistry

Potassium permanganate solution is used as a standard solution in various analytical procedures, particularly in redox titrations. It is also used as an oxidizing agent in organic synthesis and as a disinfectant. The accurate preparation and standardization of potassium permanganate solution are crucial for obtaining reliable and accurate analytical results in pharmaceutical analysis.

1.3.3.7 Ceric Ammonium Sulphate

Preparation of Ceric Ammonium Sulphate Solution

Ceric ammonium sulphate, also known as ammonium cerium(IV) sulphate ((NH_4)2Ce(SO_4)4), is a strong oxidizing agent commonly used in analytical chemistry. To prepare a standard solution of ceric ammonium sulphate, follow these steps:

1. **Weighing of Ceric Ammonium Sulphate:** Accurately weigh a known mass of ceric ammonium sulphate using an analytical balance. The mass should be appropriate for the desired concentration of the solution.

2. **Dissolution of Ceric Ammonium Sulphate:** Transfer the weighed ceric ammonium sulphate to a clean, dry beaker. Add distilled water to dissolve the ceric ammonium sulphate completely.

3. **Transfer to Volumetric Flask:** Once the ceric ammonium sulphate is completely dissolved, transfer the solution to a 1000 mL volumetric flask using a funnel. Rinse the beaker several times with distilled water to ensure all the ceric ammonium sulphate is transferred.

4. **Dilution to Volume:** Add distilled water to the volumetric flask until the bottom of the meniscus is at the mark on the neck of the flask. Use a dropper or a wash bottle for the final volume adjustment to avoid

overfilling.

5. **Mixing the Solution:** Cap the volumetric flask and invert it several times to ensure thorough mixing of the solution. This will ensure a homogenous concentration throughout the solution.

Standardization of Ceric Ammonium Sulphate Solution

After preparing the ceric ammonium sulphate solution, it needs to be standardized against a primary standard such as ferrous ammonium sulphate $((NH_4)2Fe(SO_4)2)$ to determine its exact concentration. Follow these steps for standardization:

1. **Preparation of Ferrous Ammonium Sulphate Solution:** Prepare a standard solution of ferrous ammonium sulphate of known concentration. This solution will be used as the titrant in the standardization process.
2. **Titration:** Pipette a known volume of the ferrous ammonium sulphate solution into a conical flask. Add a few drops of sulfuric acid (H2SO4) as a catalyst and titrate with the ceric ammonium sulphate solution until a color change from yellow to blue is observed.
3. **Calculation:** The volume and concentration of the ceric ammonium sulphate solution used in the titration, along with the stoichiometry of the reaction between ferrous ammonium sulphate and ceric ammonium sulphate, can be used to calculate the exact concentration of the ceric ammonium sulphate solution.

Significance of Ceric Ammonium Sulphate Solution in Analytical Chemistry

Ceric ammonium sulphate solution is used as a standard solution in various analytical procedures, particularly in redox titrations. It is also used as an oxidizing agent in organic synthesis and as a catalyst in certain reactions. The accurate preparation and standardization of ceric ammonium sulphate solution are crucial for obtaining reliable and accurate analytical results in pharmaceutical analysis.

Type	Compound	Use
Primary Standard	Sodium carbonate (Na_2CO_3)	Standardization of acids
Primary Standard	Potassium hydrogen phthalate (KHP)	Standardization of bases
Primary Standard	Silver nitrate ($AgNO_3$)	Standardization of halides
Primary Standard	Oxalic acid ($C_2H_2O_4$)	Standardization of potassium permanganate
Secondary Standard	Sodium hydroxide (NaOH)	Titrations requiring a strong base
Secondary Standard	Hydrochloric acid (HCl)	Titrations requiring a strong acid
Secondary Standard	Sodium thiosulfate ($Na_2S_2O_3$)	Iodometric titrations

Table 2: Common Primary and Secondary Standards

Solution	Preparation Method	Standardization Method
Oxalic Acid (0.1 M)	Dissolve calculated amount in water	Titrate with NaOH using phenolphthalein indicator
Sodium Hydroxide (0.1 M)	Dissolve pellets in water	Titrate with KHP using phenolphthalein indicator
Hydrochloric Acid (0.1 M)	Dilute concentrated HCl	Titrate with Na_2CO_3 using methyl orange indicator
Sodium Thiosulfate (0.1 M)	Dissolve crystals in water	Titrate with KIO_3 using starch indicator
Sulfuric Acid (0.1 M)	Dilute concentrated H_2SO_4	Titrate with NaOH using phenolphthalein indicator
Potassium Permanganate (0.1 M)	Dissolve crystals in water	Titrate with oxalic acid in the presence of heat
Ceric Ammonium Sulfate (0.1 M)	Dissolve crystals in water	Titrate with $FeSO_4$ using ferroin indicator

Table 3: Preparation and Standardization of Solutions

CHAPTER II

Errors in Pharmaceutical Analysis

Introduction

Pharmaceutical analysis is a critical field within the pharmaceutical industry, encompassing a variety of methods and techniques to ensure the quality, safety, and efficacy of drugs. The precision and accuracy of analytical results are paramount, as they directly impact drug formulation, stability, dosage, and regulatory compliance. However, achieving these high standards is often challenged by various types of errors that can occur during the analytical process. Understanding these errors, their sources, and ways to mitigate them is essential for analytical chemists and quality control professionals.

Errors in pharmaceutical analysis can be broadly categorized into two types: **systematic errors** and **random errors**. Systematic errors are consistent and predictable biases in measurement, often caused by flawed instruments or methodologies. Random errors, on the other hand, are unpredictable and arise from numerous small, uncontrollable variables. Both types of errors can significantly impact the reliability and validity of analytical data, leading to incorrect conclusions and potentially harmful consequences in drug production and patient safety.

Impact of Errors in Pharmaceutical Analysis

Errors in pharmaceutical analysis can have significant consequences, affecting everything from drug formulation to regulatory compliance. The accuracy and precision of analytical results are crucial for ensuring that drugs meet the required standards for potency, purity, and stability. Errors can lead to:

1. **Incorrect Drug Formulation:** Errors in the measurement of active pharmaceutical ingredients (APIs) can result in incorrect drug formulations, potentially leading to reduced efficacy or increased toxicity.
2. **Failed Quality Control Tests:** Systematic errors can cause batches of drugs to fail quality control tests, leading to costly delays and waste.
3. **Regulatory Non-Compliance:** Pharmaceutical companies must adhere to strict regulatory standards. Analytical errors can result in non-

compliance, leading to fines, recalls, and damage to reputation.

4. **Patient Safety Risks:** Inaccurate analysis can lead to the release of drugs with incorrect dosages or harmful impurities, posing serious risks to patient safety.

Strategies to Minimize Errors

To ensure the accuracy and precision of analytical results, it is essential to implement strategies to minimize both systematic and random errors. These strategies include:

1. **Regular Calibration and Maintenance of Instruments:** Regular calibration and maintenance of analytical instruments can help detect and correct instrumental errors. Using certified reference standards for calibration ensures that instruments provide accurate measurements.
2. **Standard Operating Procedures (SOPs):** Developing and strictly adhering to SOPs can minimize methodological errors. SOPs should include detailed instructions for each analytical procedure, ensuring consistency in how they are performed.
3. **Training and Proficiency Testing:** Regular training and proficiency testing for analysts can help reduce human-related random errors. Ensuring that all analysts are proficient in the techniques they use can improve the reliability of analytical results.
4. **Environmental Controls:** Implementing controls to maintain stable environmental conditions in the laboratory can help reduce environmental errors. This can include maintaining a consistent temperature and humidity, and minimizing electromagnetic interference.
5. **Quality Assurance Programs:** Establishing robust quality assurance programs that include regular audits, inter-laboratory comparisons, and method validation can help identify and correct sources of error.

Examples of Errors in Pharmaceutical Analysis

Instrumental Errors Example: In high-performance liquid chromatography (HPLC), if the flow rate of the mobile phase is not correctly calibrated, it can lead to systematic errors in retention times, affecting the identification and quantification of analytes. Regular calibration of the HPLC system using standard solutions can help correct this error.

Methodological Errors Example: In a titration procedure, if the endpoint is consistently overshot due to a slow reaction time, the amount of titrant added will be systematically higher. This can be corrected by improving the titration technique, such as by adding the titrant more slowly near the endpoint or using a more sensitive indicator.

Environmental Errors Example: In gravimetric analysis, variations in room temperature can cause changes in the mass of hygroscopic substances. Maintaining a controlled environment with a stable temperature and humidity can help minimize this type of error.

2.1 Types and Sources of Errors

2.1.1 Systematic Errors

Introduction to Systematic Errors

In analytical chemistry, the accuracy and precision of measurements are paramount. **Systematic errors** are a significant type of error that can affect the results of an analysis, leading to consistently biased outcomes. Unlike random errors, which vary unpredictably, systematic errors are reproducible inaccuracies that arise from identifiable sources and cause the measured values to deviate from the true value in a consistent manner.

Definition and Nature of Systematic Errors

Systematic errors, also known as determinate errors, are errors that consistently occur in the same direction—either always too high or too low. These errors are predictable and often quantifiable, making them potentially correctable once identified. They can originate from various sources including the experimental method, the measuring instruments, and the environment in which the measurements are taken.

The significance of understanding and mitigating systematic errors lies in their potential to skew experimental results and lead to incorrect conclusions. In pharmaceutical analysis, where precise and accurate measurements are critical for drug safety and efficacy, addressing systematic errors is crucial.

Sources of Systematic Errors

Systematic errors can arise from multiple sources, each contributing to the overall bias in the analytical results. These sources can be broadly categorized into three main types:

1. **Instrumental Errors**
2. **Methodological Errors**
3. **Environmental Errors**

Instrumental Errors

Instrumental errors occur due to imperfections or malfunctions in the measurement instruments themselves. These can include:

- **Calibration Errors:** If instruments are not calibrated correctly, all subsequent measurements will be consistently off by the same amount. Regular calibration against known standards is essential to minimize these errors.
- **Instrument Drift:** Over time, the performance of instruments can change, leading to drift. For example, electronic balances may show drift due to changes in temperature or humidity.
- **Zero Errors:** Instruments that do not start from a true zero can cause all measurements to be offset. Ensuring that instruments are properly zeroed before use is critical.

Example: If a balance used to measure a substance consistently reads 0.5 grams higher due to a calibration error, all measurements will be overestimated by 0.5 grams.

Methodological Errors

Methodological errors stem from flaws in the experimental procedures or techniques used. These can include:

- **Consistent Technique Flaws:** Errors arising from consistently incorrect techniques, such as pipetting inaccuracies or improper titration techniques.
- **Reagent Impurities:** Using impure reagents can lead to systematic biases in chemical reactions and measurements.
- **Assumptions and Approximations:** Simplifications or assumptions made during the method development can introduce biases. For example, assuming a reaction goes to completion when it only partially does.

Example: If a titration method consistently overshoots the endpoint due to a slow reaction time, the amount of titrant added will be systematically higher, leading to overestimation of the analyte concentration.

Environmental Errors

Environmental errors are caused by external factors that affect the measurement process. These can include:

- **Temperature and Humidity:** Variations in temperature and humidity can affect the performance of instruments and the behavior of chemicals. For instance, the volume of liquids can expand or contract with temperature changes, affecting volumetric measurements.
- **Magnetic and Electromagnetic Interference:** Instruments sensitive to magnetic or electromagnetic fields can be affected by nearby equipment or power lines.
- **Air Currents:** In highly sensitive measurements, such as those involving microbalances, air currents can cause fluctuations in weight measurements.

Example: If a laboratory is not temperature-controlled, fluctuations in temperature can cause volumetric glassware to expand or contract, leading to systematic errors in volume measurements.

Detection and Correction of Systematic Errors

Detecting systematic errors requires a combination of good laboratory practices and the use of control experiments. Here are some methods to identify and correct for systematic errors:

1. **Calibration and Standardization:** Regular calibration of instruments with certified reference standards can help detect and correct for instrumental errors.
2. **Replicate Measurements:** Performing measurements multiple times and under different conditions can help identify systematic biases.
3. **Control Samples:** Using control samples with known properties can help in comparing measured values against expected values to identify errors.
4. **Method Validation:** Validating analytical methods through recovery studies, linearity tests, and inter-laboratory comparisons can help identify methodological errors.

Example: In pharmaceutical analysis, the use of internal standards can help correct for systematic errors in chromatographic methods by providing a reference point for quantification.

Minimizing Systematic Errors

Minimizing systematic errors involves careful planning and execution of experiments. Key strategies include:

- **Regular Maintenance and Calibration:** Ensuring that instruments are regularly maintained and calibrated to avoid drift and calibration errors.
- **Training and Standard Operating Procedures (SOPs):** Providing comprehensive training to laboratory personnel and adhering to SOPs can minimize technique-related errors.
- **Environmental Controls:** Implementing controls for temperature, humidity, and other environmental factors can help reduce environmental errors.

Example: In a pharmaceutical laboratory, maintaining a controlled environment with stable temperature and humidity conditions can significantly reduce systematic errors in analytical measurements.

Impact of Systematic Errors on Pharmaceutical Analysis

In pharmaceutical analysis, the impact of systematic errors can be profound. They can lead to incorrect determination of drug potency, impurity levels, and stability, which in turn can affect the safety and efficacy of pharmaceutical products. Regulatory agencies such as the FDA and EMA emphasize the importance of minimizing systematic errors to ensure the reliability of analytical results.

Conclusion

Systematic errors represent a critical challenge in analytical chemistry, particularly in the pharmaceutical industry where accuracy and precision are paramount. Understanding the sources and types of systematic errors, along with implementing robust strategies for their detection and correction, is essential for achieving reliable and accurate analytical results. By adhering to good laboratory practices and continuously validating methods and instruments, systematic errors can be minimized, ensuring the integrity of analytical data and the safety of pharmaceutical products.

Source of Error	Type of Error	Description
Instrumental	Systematic Error	Calibration issues, instrumental drift
Procedural	Systematic Error	Incorrect procedure, contamination
Environmental	Systematic Error	Temperature fluctuations, humidity
Human	Systematic Error	Bias, incorrect measurements
Random Fluctuations	Random Error	Variations in measurements due to random factors
Reagent Impurities	Systematic Error	Impurities in reagents causing consistent deviations

Table 4: Sources and Types of Errors in Analysis

2.1 Types and Sources of Errors

2.1.2 Random Errors

Introduction to Random Errors

In the realm of pharmaceutical analysis, precision and accuracy are of utmost importance. Random errors, also known as indeterminate errors, are deviations that occur unpredictably and vary in magnitude and direction. Unlike systematic errors, which are consistent and can often be identified and corrected, random errors arise from a multitude of small, unpredictable factors that can influence the outcome of an analysis. Understanding the nature, sources, and ways to mitigate random errors is crucial for ensuring reliable and accurate analytical results.

Definition and Nature of Random Errors

Random errors are unpredictable fluctuations in the measured data that occur due to uncontrollable variables during the experimental process. These errors are inherent in all types of measurements and can be attributed to various minor and random influences. They are typically distributed symmetrically around the true value, following a normal distribution, and their effects can be minimized but not entirely eliminated.

Sources of Random Errors

Random errors can originate from several sources, broadly categorized into human factors, instrumental factors, and environmental factors. Each of these sources can introduce variability in measurements, affecting the overall precision of the analytical process.

Human Factors

Human factors play a significant role in the introduction of random errors. These include:

- **Operator Variability:** Different analysts may perform the same procedure slightly differently, leading to variations in results. For instance, slight differences in pipetting techniques or the way an endpoint in a titration is judged can introduce random errors.
- **Manual Handling:** The process of manually handling samples and reagents can introduce variability. For example, the amount of pressure applied when using a pipette or the exact timing of reagent addition can vary between measurements.

Example: When different analysts measure the same sample using a micropipette, small differences in how they handle the pipette can lead to variations in the volume delivered, introducing random errors in the measurements.

Instrumental Factors

Instrumental factors that contribute to random errors include:

- **Instrumental Noise:** Electronic noise in analytical instruments, such as fluctuations in the voltage supplied to a balance or a spectrophotometer, can cause random errors.
- **Sensitivity Limits:** The sensitivity of instruments can affect the precision of measurements. Instruments with lower sensitivity may not detect minor variations, leading to random errors.
- **Resolution:** The resolution of an instrument, or its ability to distinguish small differences in measurement, can also contribute to random errors.

Example: In a spectrophotometric analysis, electronic noise in the detector can cause fluctuations in absorbance readings, leading to random errors in the quantification of the analyte.

Environmental Factors

Environmental factors are external variables that can introduce random errors, including:

- **Temperature Variations:** Small changes in temperature can affect the performance of instruments and the behavior of chemicals, leading to variability in measurements.

- **Humidity Changes:** Variations in humidity can influence the weight of hygroscopic substances, affecting gravimetric measurements.
- **Air Currents:** Air currents in the laboratory can cause fluctuations in sensitive balance measurements.

Example: In gravimetric analysis, slight changes in room temperature can cause the weight of a sample to fluctuate, introducing random errors in the measurement.

Detection and Management of Random Errors

Detecting and managing random errors involves statistical analysis and good laboratory practices. Key strategies include:

1. **Replicate Measurements:** Performing multiple measurements of the same sample can help identify the presence of random errors. The variability in the results can be quantified using statistical measures such as standard deviation and variance.
2. **Statistical Analysis:** Analyzing the distribution of measurement data can help detect random errors. A normal distribution with a small standard deviation indicates minimal random errors, while a large standard deviation suggests significant variability.
3. **Quality Control Samples:** Using quality control samples with known properties can help monitor the precision of analytical methods. Comparing the measured values with the expected values can indicate the presence of random errors.
4. **Instrument Maintenance:** Regular maintenance and calibration of instruments can help minimize random errors caused by instrumental factors.

Example: In a pharmaceutical quality control laboratory, analysts may perform triplicate measurements of a drug sample and calculate the standard deviation of the results. A low standard deviation indicates good precision, while a high standard deviation suggests the presence of random errors.

Minimizing Random Errors

While random errors cannot be completely eliminated, their impact can be minimized through careful experimental design and execution. Strategies to minimize random errors include:

1. **Standardizing Procedures:** Implementing and adhering to standardized operating procedures (SOPs) can reduce variability in how different analysts perform the same procedure.
2. **Training and Proficiency Testing:** Regular training and proficiency testing for analysts can help ensure consistency in their techniques, reducing human-related random errors.
3. **Environmental Controls:** Maintaining stable environmental conditions, such as consistent temperature and humidity, can help minimize environmental factors that contribute to random errors.
4. **Instrument Precision:** Using high-precision instruments with low noise and high resolution can reduce the impact of instrumental random errors.

Example: In a laboratory, maintaining a stable temperature and humidity environment can help minimize random errors in gravimetric measurements of hygroscopic substances.

Impact of Random Errors on Pharmaceutical Analysis

Random errors can significantly impact the precision of analytical results, leading to variability in the data. In pharmaceutical analysis, this variability can affect the determination of drug potency, purity, and stability. The consequences of random errors include:

1. **Inconsistent Results:** Random errors can cause inconsistent results, making it difficult to draw reliable conclusions from the data.
2. **Reduced Confidence in Data:** High variability due to random errors can reduce the confidence in the analytical results, necessitating additional measurements and analyses.
3. **Increased Analytical Uncertainty:** Random errors contribute to analytical uncertainty, which can complicate the interpretation of results and compliance with regulatory standards.

Conclusion

Random errors are an unavoidable part of the analytical process in pharmaceutical analysis. They arise from various sources, including human factors, instrumental noise, and environmental variability. While random errors cannot be completely eliminated, their impact can be minimized through careful experimental design, standardization of procedures, regular training, and maintaining stable environmental conditions. By understanding and managing random errors, pharmaceutical analysts can ensure the reliability and accuracy of their results, ultimately contributing to the safety and efficacy of pharmaceutical products. The rigorous application of statistical methods and quality control measures can further enhance the precision of analytical data, supporting the overall goal of achieving high standards in pharmaceutical analysis.

2.1.3 Human Errors

Introduction to Human Errors

In pharmaceutical analysis, human errors are a significant source of variability and inaccuracy. Unlike systematic errors, which are consistent and predictable, or random errors, which arise from uncontrollable external factors, human errors are typically due to mistakes or inconsistencies in the performance of the analysts. These errors can occur at any stage of the analytical process, from sample preparation to data interpretation, and can have serious consequences for the reliability and validity of analytical results. Understanding the sources and impacts of human errors, as well as strategies to minimize them, is crucial for maintaining high standards in pharmaceutical analysis.

Definition and Nature of Human Errors

Human errors are deviations from the correct or intended performance due to mistakes, lapses, or inconsistencies by the analyst. These errors can be unintentional and can arise from a variety of factors, including lack of knowledge, fatigue, distraction, or inadequate training. Human errors can lead to both systematic and random deviations in analytical results, affecting the overall quality and reliability of the data.

Sources of Human Errors

Human errors can originate from several sources, including errors in judgment, manual handling, procedural mistakes, and communication issues. Each of these sources can introduce variability and inaccuracy in the analytical process.

Errors in Judgment

Errors in judgment occur when analysts make incorrect decisions or assumptions during the analytical process. These errors can result from a lack of experience, inadequate knowledge, or misinterpretation of data.

- **Example:** An analyst might incorrectly identify the endpoint of a titration due to misinterpretation of the color change, leading to incorrect quantification of the analyte.

Manual Handling Errors

Manual handling errors are mistakes that occur during the physical manipulation of samples and reagents. These errors can result from inconsistencies in technique, carelessness, or inadequate training.

- **Example:** Inconsistent pipetting technique, such as varying the pressure applied to the pipette plunger, can lead to variations in the volume of liquid dispensed, affecting the accuracy of the measurement.

Procedural Mistakes

Procedural mistakes occur when analysts deviate from the standard operating procedures (SOPs) or make errors in following the prescribed analytical methods. These mistakes can be due to a lack of familiarity with the procedures, inadequate training, or carelessness.

- **Example:** An analyst might omit a crucial step in the sample preparation process, such as not properly drying a sample before weighing, leading to inaccurate results.

Communication Issues

Communication issues arise when there is a lack of clear and effective communication among team members or between different departments. These issues can lead to misunderstandings, misinterpretations, and errors in the analytical process.

- **Example:** Incomplete or unclear instructions from a supervisor can lead to an analyst performing a procedure incorrectly, resulting in erroneous data.

Impact of Human Errors on Pharmaceutical Analysis

Human errors can have significant consequences in pharmaceutical analysis, affecting the accuracy, precision, and reliability of analytical results. The impact of these errors can be wide-ranging, from minor inconsistencies to major deviations that compromise the quality and safety of pharmaceutical products.

Inaccurate Results

Human errors can lead to inaccurate results, which can affect the determination of drug potency, purity, and stability. Inaccurate results can result in incorrect conclusions and decisions, potentially leading to the release of substandard or unsafe products.

- **Example:** Incorrect weighing of a sample due to human error can lead to inaccurate quantification of an active pharmaceutical ingredient (API), affecting the formulation and efficacy of the final product.

Reduced Precision

Variability introduced by human errors can reduce the precision of analytical results. This can complicate the interpretation of data and make it difficult to achieve consistent and reproducible results.

- **Example:** Variations in pipetting technique due to human error can lead to inconsistent volumes of reagents being used, resulting in reduced precision of the measurements.

Regulatory Non-Compliance

Human errors can lead to non-compliance with regulatory standards, resulting in failed quality control tests, product recalls, and regulatory penalties. Ensuring compliance with stringent regulatory requirements is critical in the pharmaceutical industry, and human errors can undermine this effort.

- **Example:** Failing to properly document analytical procedures and results due to human error can result in non-compliance with Good Laboratory Practices (GLP) and regulatory requirements.

Increased Costs and Delays

The need to repeat analyses due to human errors can increase costs and cause delays in the development and production of pharmaceutical products. This can affect the overall efficiency and profitability of pharmaceutical operations.

- **Example:** Repeating an entire analytical procedure due to an error in sample preparation can increase labor and material costs and delay the release of the final product.

Strategies to Minimize Human Errors

Minimizing human errors in pharmaceutical analysis requires a multifaceted approach, including robust training programs, standardized procedures, and effective communication. Implementing these strategies can help reduce the likelihood of human errors and improve the overall quality and reliability of analytical results.

Robust Training Programs

Comprehensive training programs are essential for ensuring that analysts are well-versed in the correct procedures and techniques. Regular training and refresher courses can help maintain high standards of performance and reduce the likelihood of errors.

- **Example:** Implementing a rigorous training program for new analysts that includes hands-on practice with analytical instruments and techniques can help ensure consistency and accuracy in their work.

Standardized Procedures

Developing and strictly adhering to standardized operating procedures (SOPs) can minimize procedural mistakes and ensure consistency in the analytical process. SOPs should be clear, detailed, and regularly updated to reflect best practices and regulatory requirements.

- **Example:** Creating detailed SOPs for each analytical procedure, including step-by-step instructions and troubleshooting tips, can help analysts perform their tasks accurately and consistently.

Effective Communication

Promoting clear and effective communication among team members and departments is crucial for minimizing misunderstandings and errors. Regular meetings, clear documentation, and open channels of communication can help ensure that everyone is on the same page.

- **Example:** Holding regular team meetings to discuss ongoing projects and potential issues can help identify and address sources of human errors before they affect the analytical results.

Automation and Technology

Leveraging automation and advanced technology can help reduce human errors by minimizing manual handling and improving precision. Automated systems and instruments can perform repetitive tasks with high accuracy and consistency.

- **Example:** Using automated pipetting systems can reduce variability in liquid handling and improve the precision of volume measurements, minimizing human errors.

Examples of Human Errors in Pharmaceutical Analysis

Example 1: Pipetting Errors

Inconsistent pipetting technique can introduce significant variability in measurements. For instance, applying different amounts of pressure to the pipette plunger can result in different volumes of liquid being dispensed, affecting the accuracy and precision of the analysis. Regular training and proficiency testing for analysts can help standardize pipetting techniques and minimize these errors.

Example 2: Weighing Errors

Errors in weighing samples can occur due to improper handling of the balance or incorrect calibration. An analyst might inadvertently place the sample incorrectly on the balance or fail to account for the buoyancy effect, leading to inaccurate weight measurements. Regular maintenance and calibration of balances, along with proper training, can help mitigate these errors.

Example 3: Titration Errors

Human errors in titration, such as misjudging the endpoint or adding titrant too quickly, can lead to incorrect quantification of the analyte. Using more sensitive indicators and implementing automated titration systems can help improve accuracy and reduce human errors in this process.

Conclusion

Human errors are an inevitable part of pharmaceutical analysis, but their impact can be minimized through careful planning, robust training programs, standardized procedures, and effective communication. By understanding the sources and consequences of human errors, analysts and quality control professionals can implement strategies to reduce their occurrence and ensure the accuracy, precision, and reliability of analytical results. The ultimate goal is to maintain high standards of quality in pharmaceutical analysis, ensuring the safety and efficacy of pharmaceutical products and compliance with regulatory requirements. Through continuous improvement and adherence to best practices, the pharmaceutical industry can minimize human errors and achieve excellence in analytical performance.

2.1.4 Instrumental Errors

Introduction to Instrumental Errors

In the realm of pharmaceutical analysis, instrumental errors are deviations that arise from the malfunction or limitations of the analytical instruments used. These errors can significantly impact the accuracy and precision of analytical results, making it crucial for analysts to understand, identify, and mitigate them. Unlike human errors, which are caused by the actions or inactions of the analyst, instrumental errors are typically due to issues with the equipment itself. These can include calibration errors, mechanical failures, or electronic malfunctions. Ensuring the proper maintenance and calibration of instruments is essential for obtaining reliable and reproducible results in pharmaceutical analysis.

Definition and Nature of Instrumental Errors

Instrumental errors are inaccuracies in measurement that occur due to the faults or limitations of the analytical instruments. These errors can be systematic, leading to consistent biases in the results, or random, causing unpredictable variations. Understanding the sources of instrumental errors and how they can affect analytical outcomes is vital for maintaining the integrity of the analysis.

Sources of Instrumental Errors

Instrumental errors can arise from various sources, including calibration issues, mechanical defects, electronic noise, and environmental factors. Each of these sources can introduce variability and inaccuracies in the analytical process.

Calibration Errors

Calibration errors occur when instruments are not properly calibrated, leading to incorrect measurements. Calibration is the process of setting an instrument to provide accurate readings, typically using known standards. Inadequate or incorrect calibration can cause systematic errors, where the instrument consistently provides biased results.

- **Example:** If a balance is not calibrated correctly, it may consistently overestimate or underestimate the weight of samples, affecting the accuracy of the results.

Mechanical Defects

Mechanical defects in instruments can cause errors in measurement due to wear and tear, damage, or manufacturing flaws. These defects can lead to systematic or random errors, depending on the nature of the defect.

- **Example:** A pipette with a worn-out piston may not dispense the correct volume of liquid, leading to inconsistent and inaccurate measurements.

Electronic Noise

Electronic noise refers to unwanted variations in the electrical signals within an instrument. This noise can interfere with the measurement process, causing random errors that affect the precision of the results.

- **Example:** Electronic noise in a spectrophotometer can cause fluctuations in the absorbance readings, affecting the precision and reliability of the measurements.

Environmental Factors

Environmental factors such as temperature, humidity, and vibrations can also contribute to instrumental errors. These factors can affect the performance of instruments, leading to variations in measurements.

- **Example:** Temperature fluctuations in the laboratory can affect the performance of sensitive instruments like balances and chromatographs, leading to variations in the results.

Impact of Instrumental Errors on Pharmaceutical Analysis

Instrumental errors can have significant consequences in pharmaceutical analysis, affecting the accuracy, precision, and reliability of analytical results. The impact of these errors can be wide-ranging, from minor inconsistencies to major deviations that compromise the quality and safety of pharmaceutical products.

Inaccurate Results

Instrumental errors can lead to inaccurate results, which can affect the determination of drug potency, purity, and stability. Inaccurate results can result in incorrect conclusions and decisions, potentially leading to the release of substandard or unsafe products.

- **Example:** An inaccurately calibrated spectrophotometer might provide incorrect absorbance readings, leading to erroneous quantification of an active pharmaceutical ingredient (API).

Reduced Precision

Variability introduced by instrumental errors can reduce the precision of analytical results. This can complicate the interpretation of data and make it difficult to achieve consistent and reproducible results.

- **Example:** Variations in the performance of a chromatographic system due to electronic noise can lead to inconsistent retention times, reducing the precision of the separation.

Regulatory Non-Compliance

Instrumental errors can lead to non-compliance with regulatory standards, resulting in failed quality control tests, product recalls, and regulatory penalties. Ensuring compliance with stringent regulatory requirements is critical in the pharmaceutical industry, and instrumental errors can undermine this effort.

- **Example:** Inaccurate measurements due to poorly maintained instruments can lead to non-compliance with Good Laboratory Practices (GLP) and regulatory requirements.

Increased Costs and Delays

The need to repeat analyses due to instrumental errors can increase costs and cause delays in the development and production of pharmaceutical products. This can affect the overall efficiency and profitability of pharmaceutical operations.

- **Example:** Repeating an entire analytical procedure due to an error in an instrument's calibration can increase labor and material costs and delay the release of the final product.

Strategies to Minimize Instrumental Errors

Minimizing instrumental errors in pharmaceutical analysis requires a multifaceted approach, including regular maintenance and calibration of instruments, proper training of analysts, and implementation of quality control measures. Implementing these strategies can help reduce the likelihood of instrumental errors and improve the overall quality and reliability of analytical results.

Regular Maintenance and Calibration

Regular maintenance and calibration of instruments are essential for ensuring their accuracy and reliability. Instruments should be calibrated using known standards and maintained according to the manufacturer's recommendations.

- **Example:** Establishing a routine maintenance schedule for all analytical instruments, including regular calibration checks and preventive maintenance, can help identify and address potential issues before they affect the results.

Proper Training of Analysts

Proper training of analysts on the correct use and maintenance of instruments is crucial for minimizing instrumental errors. Analysts should be familiar with the operation, calibration, and troubleshooting of the instruments they use.

- **Example:** Providing comprehensive training programs for analysts that include hands-on practice with the instruments and instruction on proper calibration techniques can help reduce instrumental errors.

Implementation of Quality Control Measures

Implementing quality control measures such as using control samples and conducting regular performance checks can help detect and address instrumental errors. Quality control measures can provide early warning of potential issues and ensure the accuracy and precision of the results.

- **Example:** Using control samples with known concentrations in each analytical run can help identify any deviations in instrument performance and prompt corrective actions.

Environmental Controls

Controlling environmental factors such as temperature, humidity, and vibrations in the laboratory can help minimize their impact on instrument performance. Maintaining a stable and controlled environment can reduce the likelihood of instrumental errors.

- **Example:** Installing temperature and humidity controls in the laboratory and using vibration-damping equipment can help ensure the stability and accuracy of sensitive instruments.

Examples of Instrumental Errors in Pharmaceutical Analysis

Example 1: Spectrophotometer Calibration Errors

A spectrophotometer that is not properly calibrated can provide incorrect absorbance readings, leading to inaccurate quantification of analytes. Regular calibration using standard solutions and checking the instrument's linearity can help ensure accurate measurements.

Example 2: Chromatographic System Variability

Variability in a chromatographic system, such as fluctuations in the flow rate or temperature, can affect the separation and quantification of analytes. Regular maintenance of the system, including checking and replacing worn parts, can help reduce these errors.

Example 3: Balance Drift

Balance drift occurs when the zero point of a balance changes over time, leading to inaccurate weight measurements. Regularly re-zeroing the balance and performing routine calibration checks can help ensure accurate and reliable measurements.

Conclusion

Instrumental errors are an inevitable part of pharmaceutical analysis, but their impact can be minimized through careful maintenance, proper calibration, and effective training. By understanding the sources and consequences of instrumental errors, analysts and quality control professionals can implement strategies to reduce their occurrence and ensure the accuracy, precision, and reliability of analytical results. The ultimate goal is to maintain high standards of quality in pharmaceutical analysis, ensuring the safety and efficacy of pharmaceutical products and compliance with regulatory requirements. Through continuous improvement and adherence to best practices, the pharmaceutical industry can minimize instrumental errors and achieve excellence in analytical performance.

2.2 Minimizing Errors

2.2.1 Techniques and Best Practices

In pharmaceutical analysis, minimizing errors is critical to ensure the accuracy, precision, and reliability of analytical results. Errors can arise from various sources, including human, instrumental, and methodological factors. Implementing techniques and best practices to minimize these errors is essential for maintaining high-quality standards in pharmaceutical research and production. This section discusses effective techniques and best practices for minimizing errors in pharmaceutical analysis.

Introduction to Minimizing Errors

Errors in pharmaceutical analysis can lead to inaccurate results, compromised product quality, regulatory non-compliance, and increased costs. Therefore, it is crucial to adopt strategies to identify, reduce, and control errors. By understanding the sources of errors and implementing systematic approaches to address them, analysts can enhance the reliability and robustness of their analytical procedures.

Key Techniques and Best Practices

1. Calibration and Maintenance of Instruments

Regular calibration and maintenance of analytical instruments are fundamental practices for minimizing errors. Instruments should be calibrated using certified reference materials and maintained according to the manufacturer's guidelines. This ensures that instruments provide accurate and consistent measurements.

- **Example:** A high-performance liquid chromatography (HPLC) system should undergo regular calibration with standard solutions to verify the accuracy of retention times and peak areas.

2. Standard Operating Procedures (SOPs)

Developing and adhering to standard operating procedures (SOPs) is essential for consistency and accuracy in analytical methods. SOPs provide detailed instructions for performing analytical procedures, ensuring that all analysts follow the same steps and techniques.

- **Example:** An SOP for titration might include specific guidelines for preparing reagents, performing the titration, and interpreting the results.

3. Training and Competency of Analysts

Proper training and continuous education of analysts are crucial for minimizing errors. Analysts should be well-versed in the techniques they use and understand the principles behind the methods. Regular training programs and competency assessments can help maintain high standards of analytical performance.

- **Example:** Training sessions on the correct use of a spectrophotometer, including calibration and troubleshooting, can help analysts avoid common errors.

4. Quality Control (QC) Measures

Implementing rigorous quality control measures helps identify and correct errors before they affect the final results. QC measures include using control samples, conducting regular performance checks, and running duplicate analyses to verify accuracy and precision.

- **Example:** Including a quality control sample with a known concentration in each analytical batch can help detect deviations in instrument performance.

5. Method Validation

Validating analytical methods ensures that they are suitable for their intended purpose and capable of providing accurate and reliable results. Method validation involves assessing various parameters, such as accuracy, precision, specificity, sensitivity, and robustness.

- **Example:** Validation of an assay for a new drug substance might include evaluating the linearity of the response, the limit of detection, and the reproducibility of the method across different laboratories.

6. Use of Internal Standards

Using internal standards can help compensate for variations in sample preparation and analysis, improving the accuracy and precision of quantitative measurements. An internal standard is a compound that is added to all samples, standards, and quality control samples in a consistent amount.

- **Example:** In gas chromatography, an internal standard with similar chemical properties to the analyte can be used to account for variations in sample injection and detection.

7. Environmental Controls

Controlling environmental factors such as temperature, humidity, and vibrations in the laboratory can help minimize their impact on analytical measurements. Maintaining a stable and controlled environment is especially important for sensitive instruments.

- **Example:** Using temperature-controlled environments for analytical instruments like balances and chromatographs can reduce the impact of temperature fluctuations on measurements.

8. Data Review and Verification

Implementing a thorough data review and verification process helps catch and correct errors before they affect the final results. This includes reviewing raw data, calculations, and final reports for consistency and accuracy.

- **Example:** A second analyst or supervisor reviewing the raw data and calculations for a set of assay results can help identify any discrepancies or errors that need correction.

9. Robust Sample Preparation

Ensuring robust and consistent sample preparation procedures is critical for minimizing errors in analytical results. Sample preparation should be standardized and optimized to reduce variability and improve accuracy.

- **Example:** Standardizing the procedure for extracting an active pharmaceutical ingredient from a tablet matrix can help reduce variability and improve the reliability of the results.

10. Use of Advanced Analytical Techniques

Employing advanced analytical techniques and technologies can enhance the accuracy and precision of measurements. Techniques such as mass spectrometry, nuclear magnetic resonance (NMR) spectroscopy, and advanced chromatography can provide more detailed and accurate results.

- **Example:** Using liquid chromatography-tandem mass spectrometry (LC-MS/MS) for the quantification of trace impurities in a drug product can provide higher sensitivity and specificity compared to traditional methods.

Case Studies and Examples
Case Study 1: Minimizing Errors in Titration
In a pharmaceutical laboratory, errors in titration were identified as a significant source of variability in assay results. To address this, the laboratory implemented the following best practices:

- **Calibration of burettes and pipettes:** Regular calibration and maintenance of volumetric equipment ensured accurate and consistent measurements.
- **Standardization of reagents:** Preparing and standardizing titration reagents using primary standards improved the accuracy of titration results.
- **Training analysts:** Conducting training sessions on titration techniques and error identification helped analysts minimize procedural errors.

Case Study 2: Reducing Variability in Chromatographic Analysis
A pharmaceutical company observed high variability in chromatographic analysis results due to environmental factors and instrument performance. The following measures were taken to reduce variability:

- **Environmental controls:** Implementing temperature and humidity controls in the laboratory reduced the impact of environmental fluctuations on chromatographic performance.
- **Regular instrument maintenance:** Establishing a routine maintenance schedule for chromatographic systems improved instrument reliability and performance.
- **Use of internal standards:** Incorporating internal standards in all analyses helped compensate for variations in sample preparation and analysis.

Conclusion
Minimizing errors in pharmaceutical analysis is essential for ensuring the accuracy, precision, and reliability of analytical results. By implementing techniques and best practices such as regular calibration and maintenance of instruments, developing and adhering to SOPs, proper

training of analysts, rigorous quality control measures, and robust method validation, analysts can significantly reduce the occurrence of errors. Additionally, controlling environmental factors, using internal standards, and employing advanced analytical techniques further enhance the quality of analytical results. Through continuous improvement and adherence to best practices, the pharmaceutical industry can achieve excellence in analytical performance, ensuring the safety, efficacy, and quality of pharmaceutical products.

2.2.2 Calibration and Maintenance of Instruments

In the realm of pharmaceutical analysis, the calibration and maintenance of instruments play a crucial role in ensuring the accuracy, precision, and reliability of analytical results. Instruments used in analytical chemistry are sophisticated and sensitive, requiring meticulous care and regular calibration to maintain their performance. This section delves into the importance, methods, and best practices for the calibration and maintenance of analytical instruments.

Introduction to Calibration and Maintenance

Calibration is the process of configuring an instrument to provide a result for a sample within an acceptable range. It involves comparing the measurements from an instrument against a standard with known values and making adjustments as necessary to achieve accurate readings. Maintenance, on the other hand, includes routine checks, cleaning, repairs, and replacement of parts to ensure the instrument operates efficiently and consistently.

The accuracy and precision of analytical results heavily depend on the proper calibration and maintenance of instruments. Neglecting these practices can lead to erroneous data, which in turn can affect the quality and safety of pharmaceutical products.

Importance of Calibration and Maintenance

1. Ensuring Accuracy and Precision

Calibration aligns the instrument's measurements with standard reference values, ensuring that the results are both accurate (close to the true value) and precise (consistent upon repeated measurements). This is fundamental in pharmaceutical analysis where even minor deviations can lead to significant consequences.

- **Example:** In high-performance liquid chromatography (HPLC), accurate calibration of the detector ensures that the concentration of active pharmaceutical ingredients (APIs) is measured correctly, which is vital for dosage accuracy.

2. Compliance with Regulatory Standards

Regulatory bodies such as the FDA, EMA, and ICH mandate strict calibration and maintenance protocols. Compliance with these standards is essential for the approval and continued manufacture of pharmaceutical products.

- **Example:** Good Laboratory Practice (GLP) and Good Manufacturing Practice (GMP) guidelines require documented evidence of regular calibration and maintenance of analytical instruments.

3. Enhancing Instrument Longevity

Regular maintenance extends the lifespan of analytical instruments by preventing breakdowns and ensuring they operate efficiently. This reduces the need for frequent replacements and repairs, leading to cost savings.

- **Example:** Routine cleaning and part replacement in a mass spectrometer can prevent the build-up of contaminants, which can impair the instrument's performance over time.

4. Minimizing Downtime and Operational Disruptions

Scheduled maintenance prevents unexpected instrument failures, which can cause significant disruptions in laboratory operations. By proactively addressing potential issues, laboratories can maintain continuous workflows.

- **Example:** Regular maintenance of a gas chromatograph prevents downtime due to issues like column degradation or detector malfunction, ensuring consistent productivity.

Methods of Calibration
1. Primary Calibration

Primary calibration involves using a standard that is directly traceable to a primary reference, often provided by national metrology institutes. These standards have a known and precise value, ensuring high accuracy in calibration.

- **Example:** Using a primary standard solution of sodium chloride for calibrating a conductivity meter.

2. Secondary Calibration

Secondary calibration uses a reference standard that has been calibrated against a primary standard. While slightly less accurate than primary calibration, it is widely used due to its practicality and cost-effectiveness.

- **Example:** Calibrating a pH meter using buffer solutions that have been standardized against a primary pH standard.

3. Internal Calibration

Internal calibration utilizes standards within the instrument itself. This method is convenient and allows for frequent calibration checks without external references.

- **Example:** Using an internal standard in mass spectrometry to calibrate the instrument's response.

Best Practices for Calibration
1. Regular Calibration Schedule

Establishing a regular calibration schedule based on the instrument's usage frequency and manufacturer's recommendations ensures consistent performance. Instruments should be calibrated before initial use, after significant repairs, and at regular intervals.

- **Example:** Calibrating a spectrophotometer monthly or after any major maintenance work.

2. Documentation and Record Keeping

Maintaining detailed records of calibration activities, including dates, standards used, results, and any adjustments made, is essential for traceability and compliance with regulatory requirements.

- **Example:** Keeping a calibration log for each instrument, noting the calibration standards, results, and any corrective actions taken.

3. Using Certified Reference Materials (CRMs)

Certified reference materials provide traceable and reliable standards for calibration, ensuring the accuracy and comparability of results.

- **Example:** Using certified glucose solutions for calibrating a glucose analyzer in quality control laboratories.

4. Performing Calibration Checks

Regular calibration checks between full calibrations help verify that the instrument remains within acceptable performance limits. Any deviations can be addressed promptly.

- **Example:** Running a known standard solution daily to check the calibration of an HPLC system.

Maintenance Procedures
1. Routine Cleaning

Regular cleaning of instruments prevents the build-up of contaminants that can affect performance. Cleaning protocols should be specific to each instrument and include guidelines for disassembly, cleaning agents, and reassembly.

- **Example:** Cleaning the injection port and detector of a gas chromatograph to remove residues that can cause baseline noise.

2. Replacement of Consumables

Consumable parts, such as filters, columns, and seals, should be replaced according to the manufacturer's recommendations or when signs of wear and tear are evident. This prevents instrument malfunction and maintains optimal performance.

- **Example:** Replacing the column in an HPLC system when peak resolution deteriorates.

3. Preventive Maintenance

Preventive maintenance includes scheduled activities designed to prevent instrument failure and extend its operational life. This involves inspecting, testing, and servicing critical components.

- **Example:** Regularly inspecting and replacing the pump seals in a liquid chromatography system to prevent leaks and maintain pressure stability.

4. Calibration and Adjustment of Components

Certain components of instruments, such as sensors and detectors, may require periodic calibration and adjustment to maintain their accuracy and sensitivity.

- **Example:** Calibrating the wavelength accuracy of a UV-Vis spectrophotometer using holmium oxide filters.

5. Software Updates and Validation

Updating and validating the instrument's software ensures compatibility with the latest standards and improves functionality. Software validation confirms that the updates do not negatively impact instrument performance.

- **Example:** Installing the latest software updates for a mass spectrometer and validating its performance with standard samples.

Conclusion

Calibration and maintenance of instruments are indispensable practices in pharmaceutical analysis. They ensure the accuracy, precision, and reliability of analytical results, compliance with regulatory standards, and longevity of instruments. By implementing regular calibration schedules, maintaining detailed records, using certified reference materials, performing calibration checks, and following rigorous maintenance procedures, laboratories can minimize errors and achieve high-quality analytical performance. Continuous attention to these practices is essential for the successful and efficient operation of pharmaceutical laboratories, ultimately contributing to the safety and efficacy of pharmaceutical products.

2.3.1 Definitions

Accuracy, precision, and significant figures are fundamental concepts in pharmaceutical analysis that ensure the reliability and consistency of analytical results. Understanding and correctly applying these concepts are essential for producing valid data, making informed decisions, and maintaining regulatory compliance in the pharmaceutical industry.

Accuracy

Accuracy refers to how close a measured value is to the true or accepted value. It is an indication of the correctness of a measurement. High accuracy means that the measurement results are very close to the true value, while low accuracy indicates a significant deviation from the true value.

Example: If the true concentration of a solution is 10.0 mg/mL and the measured concentration is 9.8 mg/mL, the measurement is fairly accurate. If the measured concentration were 7.0 mg/mL, the accuracy would be much lower.

- **Importance in Pharmaceutical Analysis:** Accuracy is crucial in pharmaceutical analysis because it ensures that the dosage of active ingredients in medications is correct, which directly affects their efficacy and safety. For instance, inaccurate measurements in the formulation of drugs can lead to underdosing or overdosing, potentially causing therapeutic failure or adverse effects.

Methods to Determine Accuracy:

1. **Recovery Studies:** These involve adding a known quantity of a standard to the sample and measuring the amount recovered. The percentage recovery indicates the accuracy of the analytical method.
2. **Comparison with Reference Methods:** Results obtained from the method under investigation are compared with results from a recognized reference method. The closeness of the results indicates the accuracy.

Precision

Precision refers to the consistency of measurement results when repeated under the same conditions. It indicates the reproducibility of a measurement. High precision means that repeated measurements yield very similar results, while low precision indicates significant variability.

Example: If the concentration of a solution is measured several times and the results are 10.0 mg/mL, 10.1 mg/mL, and 9.9 mg/mL, the precision is high. If the results are 10.0 mg/mL, 8.0 mg/mL, and 12.0 mg/mL, the precision is low.

- **Importance in Pharmaceutical Analysis:** Precision is vital for ensuring the reproducibility and reliability of analytical results. Consistent results are necessary for quality control and assurance in pharmaceutical manufacturing, where the same procedures must yield the same outcomes every time to maintain product quality and safety.

Types of Precision:

1. **Repeatability:** The precision of measurements under the same conditions over a short period. It is often assessed by performing multiple measurments on the same sample using the same instrument and operator.
2. **Intermediate Precision:** The precision of measurements within the same laboratory but under different conditions, such as different days, analysts, or equipment.
3. **Reproducibility:** The precision of measurements across different laboratories. It is assessed by comparing the results obtained from the same sample analyzed in multiple labs.

Significant Figures

Significant figures are the digits in a measurement that carry meaningful information about its precision. They include all the certain digits and the first uncertain digit in a measurement.

Example: In the measurement 12.345, all five digits are significant. In the measurement 0.00456, the significant figures are 4, 5, and 6.

- **Importance in Pharmaceutical Analysis:** Using the correct number of significant figures is crucial in reporting analytical results. It ensures that the reported data reflects the true precision of the measurements and avoids overestimating the accuracy of the results. In pharmaceutical analysis, significant figures help in maintaining consistency and reliability in data reporting, which is essential for regulatory compliance and scientific communication.

Rules for Determining Significant Figures:

1. **Non-Zero Digits:** All non-zero digits are significant. (e.g., 123 has three significant figures)
2. **Leading Zeros:** Leading zeros are not significant. (e.g., 0.00123 has three significant figures)

3. **Captive Zeros:** Zeros between non-zero digits are significant. (e.g., 1023 has four significant figures)
4. **Trailing Zeros:** Trailing zeros in a number with a decimal point are significant. (e.g., 12.300 has five significant figures)

Application in Pharmaceutical Analysis:

1. **Reporting Results:** Analytical results should be reported with the appropriate number of significant figures to reflect the precision of the measurement. Over-reporting or under-reporting significant figures can misrepresent the data's accuracy and precision.
2. **Calculations:** When performing calculations, the number of significant figures in the result should be consistent with the number of significant figures in the measurements used. This ensures that the calculated values are as precise as the measured data.

Conclusion

Understanding and applying the concepts of accuracy, precision, and significant figures are essential for producing reliable and consistent analytical results in pharmaceutical analysis. These principles ensure that the measurements are close to the true values (accuracy), reproducible (precision), and correctly reported (significant figures). By adhering to these practices, pharmaceutical analysts can maintain the quality and safety of pharmaceutical products, comply with regulatory standards, and contribute to the advancement of scientific knowledge.

2.3.2 Methods to Ensure Accuracy and Precision

Ensuring accuracy and precision in pharmaceutical analysis is paramount to guarantee reliable and consistent results. Various methods and practices are employed to achieve these goals, ranging from meticulous laboratory techniques to advanced instrumentation. This section discusses some key methods used to ensure accuracy and precision in pharmaceutical analysis.

1. Calibration of Instruments

Calibrating instruments regularly using certified reference materials (CRMs) or primary standards is crucial for maintaining accuracy. Calibration verifies the instrument's measurements against known standards and corrects any deviations, ensuring accurate results.

Example: Calibrating a balance using standard weights to ensure accurate measurement of sample weights.

2. Quality Control Checks

Implementing robust quality control (QC) measures helps monitor and maintain precision. Using control samples with known concentrations or properties allows analysts to assess the precision of their measurements and identify any deviations.

Example: Running a control sample alongside samples in an analytical run to verify the precision of the method.

3. Standard Operating Procedures (SOPs)

Following **standard operating procedures** for analytical methods ensures consistency and precision in measurements. SOPs provide step-by-step instructions for sample preparation, analysis, and data interpretation.

Example: Using an SOP for HPLC analysis that specifies the mobile phase composition, flow rate, column temperature, and detector settings.

4. Training and Competency

Training analysts in proper laboratory techniques and instrument operation is essential for ensuring accuracy and precision. Competent analysts are more likely to perform measurements correctly and identify potential sources of error.

Example: Providing hands-on training to analysts on pipetting techniques to improve accuracy in volumetric measurements.

5. Method Validation

Validating analytical methods to ensure they are suitable for their intended use is critical for accuracy and precision. Method validation involves assessing parameters such as accuracy, precision, specificity, and robustness.

Example: Validating an assay method for a drug to ensure it accurately measures the drug's concentration in a dosage form.

6. Environmental Controls

Controlling environmental conditions such as temperature, humidity, and light exposure can help maintain the accuracy and precision of measurements. Fluctuations in environmental conditions can affect instrument performance and sample stability.

Example: Using a temperature-controlled room for storing reference standards to prevent degradation.

7. Data Handling and Analysis

Implementing proper data handling and analysis techniques can improve accuracy and precision. This includes using appropriate statistical methods to analyze data and identify outliers or trends.

Example: Using statistical software to analyze chromatographic data and calculate peak areas accurately.

8. Regular Maintenance and Cleaning

Regular maintenance and cleaning of instruments help ensure their accuracy and precision. This includes cleaning optics, replacing worn parts, and calibrating sensors.

Example: Cleaning the detector window of a spectrophotometer to ensure accurate measurement of absorbance.

9. Use of Internal Standards

Using internal standards in analytical methods can improve accuracy and precision by accounting for variations in sample preparation and analysis.

Example: Adding a known amount of an internal standard to a sample before analysis to correct for variations in injection volume or detector response.

10. Peer Review and Audit

Conducting regular peer reviews and audits of analytical procedures can help identify potential sources of error and ensure that best practices are being followed.

Example: Having a second analyst review and verify analytical data before finalizing the results.

Conclusion

Ensuring accuracy and precision in pharmaceutical analysis requires a combination of proper techniques, instrumentation, and laboratory practices. By following rigorous calibration procedures, implementing robust quality control measures, adhering to SOPs, and maintaining a high level of training and competency among analysts, pharmaceutical laboratories can produce reliable and consistent results. These practices are essential for maintaining the quality, safety, and efficacy of pharmaceutical products.

2.3.3 Use of Significant Figures

Significant figures play a crucial role in expressing the precision of measured values in pharmaceutical analysis. Understanding how to determine and use significant figures correctly is essential for accurately reporting analytical results. This section explains the concept of significant figures and provides guidelines for their proper use in pharmaceutical analysis.

Definition of Significant Figures

Significant figures are the digits in a numerical value that carry meaning regarding its precision. They include all certain digits and the first uncertain digit in a measurement. The number of significant figures indicates the precision of a measurement.

Example: In the measurement 12.345, there are five significant figures (1, 2, 3, 4, and 5). In the measurement 0.00456, there are three significant figures (4, 5, and 6).

Guidelines for Using Significant Figures

1. **Non-Zero Digits:** All non-zero digits are significant.

   ◦ Example: 123 has three significant figures.

2. **Leading Zeros:** Leading zeros are not significant.

   ◦ Example: 0.00123 has three significant figures.

3. **Captive Zeros:** Zeros between non-zero digits are significant.

   ◦ Example: 1023 has four significant figures.

4. **Trailing Zeros:** Trailing zeros in a number with a decimal point are significant.

   ◦ Example: 12.300 has five significant figures.

Rule	Example
Non-zero digits are always significant	123.45 has 5 significant figures
Any zeros between significant digits are significant	1002 has 4 significant figures
Leading zeros are not significant	0.00123 has 3 significant figures
Trailing zeros in a decimal number are significant	123.4500 has 7 significant figures
Trailing zeros in a whole number without a decimal point are not significant	1000 has 1 significant figure (unless specified with a decimal point as in 1000. has 4 significant figures)

Table 5: Rules for Significant Figures

Significance in Pharmaceutical Analysis

1. Reporting Results: When reporting analytical results, it is important to use the appropriate number of significant figures to reflect the precision of the measurement. Over-reporting or under-reporting significant figures can lead to inaccurate representation of the data's precision.

2. Calculations: When performing calculations with measured values, the result should be rounded to the same number of significant figures as the least precise measurement used in the calculation. This ensures that the calculated result is not more precise than the original measurements.

Example: If the measurements used in a calculation are 10.2, 5.41, and 3.0, the result should be rounded to two decimal places (the least precise measurement).

3. Conversion Factors: When using conversion factors in calculations, the number of significant figures in the conversion factor should not affect the number of significant figures in the final result.

Example: Converting 1.2345 grams to milligrams (1 g = 1000 mg) should result in 1234.5 mg, with five significant figures.

4. Analytical Methods: In analytical methods where precision is critical, such as high-performance liquid chromatography (HPLC) or mass spectrometry, maintaining the correct number of significant figures is essential for accurately determining the concentration or purity of a sample.

Conclusion

Understanding and correctly applying the rules for significant figures are essential for expressing the precision of measurements in pharmaceutical analysis. By following these guidelines, analysts can ensure that their results are reported accurately and that the precision of the measurements is correctly represented. This is crucial for maintaining the quality and reliability of analytical data in the pharmaceutical industry.

CHAPTER III

Pharmacopoeias and Impurities

Pharmacopoeias and Impurities in Pharmaceutical Analysis

Pharmacopoeias are authoritative books that contain a compilation of standards and guidelines for the identification, quality, purity, and strength of drugs and pharmaceutical substances. These standards are essential for ensuring the safety, efficacy, and quality of pharmaceutical products. One crucial aspect covered in pharmacopoeias is the identification and control of impurities in pharmaceutical substances. Impurities can arise from various sources during the manufacturing, storage, or handling of drugs, and their presence can affect the quality and safety of pharmaceutical products. This section explores the role of pharmacopoeias in the control of impurities and their significance in pharmaceutical analysis.

Introduction to Pharmacopoeias

Pharmacopoeias are official compendia recognized by regulatory authorities and used by pharmaceutical manufacturers, regulatory agencies, and healthcare professionals to ensure the quality and safety of drugs. They provide detailed monographs for each drug, including information on its physical and chemical properties, identification tests, purity requirements, and dosage forms. Pharmacopoeias also establish standards for the testing and analysis of drugs, including methods for the detection and quantification of impurities.

Significance of Pharmacopoeial Standards

Pharmacopoeial standards serve several important functions in pharmaceutical analysis:

1. **Quality Assurance:** Pharmacopoeial standards ensure that pharmaceutical products meet specific quality criteria, including purity, potency, and stability. Compliance with these standards is essential for regulatory approval and market acceptance.

2. **Safety:** Pharmacopoeial standards help ensure the safety of pharmaceutical products by setting limits for impurities that may be

harmful to health. These limits are based on scientific evidence and toxicological data.

3. **Interchangeability:** Pharmacopoeial standards facilitate the interchangeability of pharmaceutical products by ensuring consistency in quality and performance. This is particularly important for generic drugs, where bioequivalence is crucial.

4. **International Harmonization:** Many pharmacopoeias are recognized internationally, promoting harmonization of standards across different countries and regions. This harmonization simplifies regulatory compliance for multinational pharmaceutical companies.

Types of Impurities

Impurities in pharmaceutical substances can be classified into several categories based on their origin and impact on product quality:

1. **Organic Impurities:** Organic impurities can arise from starting materials, intermediates, or degradation products. They are typically controlled using chromatographic methods such as HPLC or GC.

2. **Inorganic Impurities:** Inorganic impurities can include metals, metalloids, and other inorganic substances. They are controlled using techniques such as atomic absorption spectroscopy (AAS) or inductively coupled plasma (ICP) analysis.

3. **Residual Solvents:** Residual solvents are used during the manufacturing process and must be controlled to ensure product safety. They are typically analyzed using gas chromatography (GC).

4. **Microbial Impurities:** Microbial impurities can include bacteria, fungi, and other microorganisms. They are controlled through microbial limit tests and sterility testing.

Control of Impurities in Pharmacopoeias

Pharmacopoeias provide detailed guidelines for the control of impurities in pharmaceutical substances, including:

1. **Identification Tests:** Pharmacopoeial monographs include specific identification tests to ensure the identity of a pharmaceutical substance and detect the presence of impurities.

2. **Limit Tests:** Pharmacopoeial standards set limits for specific impurities based on their toxicity and potential impact on product quality. These

limits must be met for a product to comply with pharmacopoeial standards.

3. **Analytical Methods:** Pharmacopoeias describe validated analytical methods for the detection and quantification of impurities, ensuring the accuracy and reliability of impurity testing.

4. **Validation of Methods:** Pharmacopoeias require that analytical methods used for impurity testing be validated to demonstrate their accuracy, precision, specificity, and robustness.

Pharmacopoeias play a crucial role in the control of impurities in pharmaceutical substances. By providing standards and guidelines for the identification, testing, and control of impurities, pharmacopoeias ensure the quality, safety, and efficacy of pharmaceutical products. Compliance with pharmacopoeial standards is essential for pharmaceutical manufacturers to meet regulatory requirements and ensure the quality of their products.

3.1 Overview of Major Pharmacopoeias

Pharmacopoeias are authoritative books that contain standards and guidelines for the quality, purity, and strength of drugs and pharmaceutical substances. They play a crucial role in ensuring the safety, efficacy, and quality of pharmaceutical products. Several major pharmacopoeias are used worldwide, each with its own set of standards and guidelines. This section provides an overview of some of the major pharmacopoeias, including the United States Pharmacopeia (USP), the European Pharmacopoeia (Ph. Eur.), and the Indian Pharmacopoeia (IP).

3.1.1 United States Pharmacopeia (USP)

The United States Pharmacopeia (USP) is one of the most widely used pharmacopoeias in the world. It contains standards for the quality, purity, strength, and consistency of drugs and pharmaceutical substances marketed in the United States. The USP is recognized by the U.S. Food and Drug Administration (FDA) as the official compendium for drug standards in the United States.

History and Development: The USP was first published in 1820 and has since undergone several revisions and updates to reflect advances in pharmaceutical science and technology. It is published by the United States Pharmacopeial Convention (USP), a nonprofit organization that sets standards for the identity, strength, quality, and purity of medicines.

Content and Standards: The USP contains monographs for drug substances, dosage forms, and compounded preparations. Each monograph includes specifications for the identity, purity, and quality of the drug, as well as analytical methods for testing these attributes. The USP also includes general chapters on topics such as pharmaceutical dosage forms, packaging, and storage conditions.

Regulatory Status: Compliance with the standards set forth in the USP is required by the FDA for drugs marketed in the United States. The USP-NF (National Formulary) is recognized as the official compendium for drug standards under the Federal Food, Drug, and Cosmetic Act.

International Recognition: The USP is recognized and used in many countries around the world as a reference standard for drug quality and purity. It is also used by the World Health Organization (WHO) as a basis for the development of pharmacopoeial standards in other countries.

3.1.2 British Pharmacopoeia (BP)

The British Pharmacopoeia (BP) is an authoritative compendium of quality standards for medicinal products in the United Kingdom (UK) and is widely used internationally. It provides standards for the quality, safety, and efficacy of pharmaceutical substances and dosage forms, ensuring that medicines meet the required standards of purity, strength, and quality. This section provides an overview of the British Pharmacopoeia, its history, content, and significance in pharmaceutical regulation and practice.

History and Development: The British Pharmacopoeia was first published in 1864 and has since been revised and updated regularly to reflect advances in pharmaceutical science and technology. It is published by the British Pharmacopoeia Commission, which is part of the Medicines and Healthcare products Regulatory Agency (MHRA) in the UK.

Content and Standards: The British Pharmacopoeia contains monographs for pharmaceutical substances, dosage forms, and compounded preparations. Each monograph includes specifications for the identity, purity, and quality of the drug, as well as analytical methods for testing these attributes. The BP also includes general chapters on topics such as pharmaceutical dosage forms, packaging, and storage conditions.

Regulatory Status: Compliance with the standards set forth in the British Pharmacopoeia is required by law in the UK for medicinal products. The BP is also recognized internationally and is used as a reference standard for drug quality and purity in many countries around the world.

International Recognition: The British Pharmacopoeia is recognized internationally and is used as a reference standard for drug quality and purity in many countries around the world. It is also used by the World Health Organization (WHO) as a basis for the development of pharmacopoeial standards in other countries.

3.1.3 Indian Pharmacopoeia (IP)

The Indian Pharmacopoeia (IP) is an official compendium of standards for pharmaceutical substances and dosage forms used in India. It contains guidelines for the quality, safety, and efficacy of drugs and pharmaceuticals marketed in India, ensuring that they meet the required standards of purity, strength, and quality. This section provides an overview of the Indian Pharmacopoeia, its history, content, and significance in pharmaceutical regulation and practice.

History and Development: The Indian Pharmacopoeia was first published in 1955 and has since been revised and updated regularly to reflect advances in pharmaceutical science and technology. It is published by the Indian Pharmacopoeia Commission (IPC), which operates under the Ministry of Health and Family Welfare, Government of India.

Content and Standards: The Indian Pharmacopoeia contains monographs for pharmaceutical substances, dosage forms, and compounded preparations. Each monograph includes specifications for the identity, purity, and quality of the drug, as well as analytical methods for testing these attributes. The IP also includes general chapters on topics such as pharmaceutical dosage forms, packaging, and storage conditions.

Regulatory Status: Compliance with the standards set forth in the Indian Pharmacopoeia is required by law in India for medicinal products. The IP is also recognized internationally and is used as a reference standard for drug quality and purity in many countries around the world.

International Recognition: The Indian Pharmacopoeia is recognized internationally and is used as a reference standard for drug quality and purity in many countries around the world. It is also used by the World Health Organization (WHO) as a basis for the development of pharmacopoeial standards in other countries.

Conclusion

The Indian Pharmacopoeia (IP) is an essential reference for pharmaceutical manufacturers, regulatory authorities, and healthcare professionals in India and internationally. Its standards for the quality, purity, and strength of medicinal products help ensure the safety and efficacy of medicines and promote public health.

3.2 Sources of Impurities in Medicinal Agents

In pharmaceutical manufacturing, impurities can arise from various sources, including raw materials, manufacturing processes, and storage conditions. Understanding the sources of impurities is crucial for developing effective strategies to control and minimize their presence in medicinal agents. This section provides an overview of the sources of impurities in medicinal agents, highlighting the importance of quality control measures in pharmaceutical manufacturing.

3.2.1 Manufacturing Processes

The manufacturing processes involved in the production of medicinal agents can introduce impurities at various stages. These impurities can arise from reactions between raw materials, intermediates, and the environment. Common sources of impurities in manufacturing processes include:

1. **Chemical Reactions:** The chemical reactions used to synthesize medicinal agents can sometimes produce impurities as by-products. These impurities may result from side reactions, incomplete reactions, or degradation of the product.
2. **Raw Materials:** Impurities present in raw materials, such as starting materials, solvents, and reagents, can carry over into the final product. Contaminated raw materials can introduce impurities that affect the quality and purity of the medicinal agent.
3. **Equipment and Containers:** Equipment used in manufacturing, such as reactors, vessels, and pipelines, can introduce impurities if not properly cleaned and maintained. Contaminants from equipment surfaces or container closures can leach into the product.
4. **Processing Aids:** Some processing aids, such as catalysts, filters, and adsorbents, can introduce impurities if not properly controlled. These impurities can affect the quality and stability of the final product.
5. **Environmental Factors:** Environmental conditions, such as temperature, humidity, and air quality, can also impact the formation of impurities. Poor environmental control can lead to contamination of the product during manufacturing.

Controlling impurities in manufacturing processes requires careful monitoring and control of raw materials, process parameters, and equipment. Quality control measures, such as regular testing and analysis, can help identify and mitigate sources of impurities to ensure the quality and safety of medicinal agents.

3.2.3 Environmental Factors

Environmental factors play a significant role in the formation of impurities in medicinal agents during manufacturing and storage. Various environmental conditions can contribute to the degradation of pharmaceutical products, leading to the formation of impurities. Some of the key environmental factors include:

1. **Temperature:** High temperatures can accelerate chemical reactions, leading to the degradation of medicinal agents and the formation of impurities. Temperature control is crucial to prevent degradation and maintain product stability.

2. **Humidity:** High humidity can lead to the absorption of moisture by pharmaceutical products, which can cause physical and chemical changes. Moisture-sensitive products are particularly susceptible to degradation in humid conditions.

3. **Light:** Exposure to light, especially ultraviolet (UV) light, can promote the degradation of medicinal agents. Light-sensitive products should be protected from direct light exposure to prevent degradation.

4. **Air Quality:** The quality of the air in manufacturing and storage areas can affect the stability of pharmaceutical products. Contaminants in the air, such as dust, particulates, and gases, can contribute to the formation of impurities in medicinal agents.

5. **Storage Conditions:** Improper storage conditions, such as exposure to extreme temperatures, humidity, or light, can accelerate the degradation of pharmaceutical products and lead to the formation of impurities. Proper storage conditions are essential to maintain product stability.

Controlling environmental factors requires implementing appropriate measures, such as temperature and humidity control, light protection, and air quality monitoring. These measures help prevent the formation of impurities and ensure the quality and stability of medicinal agents throughout their shelf life.

3.2.2 Storage and Handling of Medicinal Agents

The storage and handling of medicinal agents are critical aspects of pharmaceutical manufacturing and distribution. Proper storage and handling practices are essential to maintain the quality, safety, and efficacy of medicinal agents throughout their shelf life. This section provides an overview of the importance of storage and handling practices, the factors that can affect the stability of medicinal agents, and the guidelines for proper storage and handling.

Introduction

Medicinal agents are susceptible to degradation and loss of potency if not stored and handled properly. Factors such as temperature, humidity, light, and environmental contaminants can affect the stability of medicinal agents, leading to the formation of impurities and loss of efficacy. Proper storage and handling practices are essential to ensure that medicinal agents retain their quality and potency throughout their shelf life.

Factors Affecting Stability

1. **Temperature:** Temperature control is crucial for maintaining the stability of medicinal agents. Excessive heat or cold can accelerate degradation reactions, leading to the formation of impurities and loss of potency.
2. **Humidity:** High humidity can promote the growth of microorganisms and lead to the degradation of medicinal agents. Moisture-sensitive products are particularly susceptible to degradation in humid conditions.
3. **Light:** Exposure to light, especially ultraviolet (UV) light, can degrade medicinal agents and lead to the formation of impurities. Light-sensitive products should be protected from direct light exposure.
4. **Environmental Contaminants:** Contaminants in the air, such as dust, particulates, and gases, can affect the stability of medicinal agents. Proper air filtration and control of environmental contaminants are essential for maintaining product quality.

Guidelines for Storage and Handling

1. **Temperature Control:** Store medicinal agents in a cool, dry place away from direct sunlight and heat sources. Follow the manufacturer's recommendations for storage temperature.
2. **Humidity Control:** Store medicinal agents in a dry environment to prevent moisture absorption. Use desiccants or humidity-controlled storage areas for moisture-sensitive products.
3. **Light Protection:** Store light-sensitive products in opaque containers or packaging to protect them from exposure to light. Use light-blocking

materials or packaging when necessary.

4. **Air Quality Control:** Ensure proper ventilation and air filtration in storage areas to minimize exposure to environmental contaminants. Use air filtration systems to maintain air quality.

5. **Packaging and Labeling:** Use appropriate packaging materials and labeling to ensure the integrity of medicinal agents during storage and handling. Follow guidelines for storage temperature, expiration date, and handling instructions.

Conclusion

Proper storage and handling practices are essential for maintaining the quality, safety, and efficacy of medicinal agents. By following guidelines for temperature control, humidity control, light protection, and air quality control, pharmaceutical manufacturers and distributors can ensure that medicinal agents retain their quality and potency throughout their shelf life.

3.3 Limit Tests in Pharmaceutical Analysis

Limit tests are analytical procedures used to determine the presence or absence of specified impurities or substances in pharmaceutical substances and dosage forms. These tests are designed to ensure that the levels of impurities or substances do not exceed predetermined limits set by regulatory authorities. Limit tests play a crucial role in pharmaceutical analysis, helping to ensure the quality, safety, and efficacy of medicinal products. This section provides an overview of limit tests, their significance in pharmaceutical analysis, and the guidelines for conducting these tests.

Introduction

Limit tests are qualitative or semi-quantitative tests that are used to detect the presence of impurities or substances at or above a specified limit. These tests are based on specific chemical reactions or physical properties of the impurities or substances being tested. Limit tests are used to verify compliance with regulatory standards and specifications for pharmaceutical products.

Significance of Limit Tests

Limit tests are essential for ensuring the quality, safety, and efficacy of pharmaceutical products. By detecting and quantifying impurities or substances at specified limits, limit tests help to:

1. **Ensure Compliance:** Limit tests ensure that pharmaceutical products comply with regulatory standards and specifications, which specify the maximum allowable levels of impurities or substances.
2. **Verify Purity:** Limit tests verify the purity of pharmaceutical substances and dosage forms by detecting the presence of impurities at specified limits.
3. **Assess Stability:** Limit tests can be used to assess the stability of pharmaceutical products by monitoring the levels of impurities over time.
4. **Ensure Safety:** Limit tests help to ensure the safety of pharmaceutical products by detecting harmful impurities or substances that may pose a risk to health.

Guidelines for Conducting Limit Tests

1. **Selection of Method:** Choose an appropriate method for conducting the limit test based on the nature of the impurity or substance being tested. Common methods include chromatographic, spectroscopic, and titrimetric methods.
2. **Sample Preparation:** Prepare the sample according to the specified procedure, ensuring that the sample is representative of the entire batch.
3. **Test Procedure:** Perform the test procedure according to the specified method, following all instructions carefully to ensure accurate results.
4. **Limit Calculation:** Calculate the limit for the impurity or substance based on the specified criteria, taking into account factors such as the dosage form, route of administration, and patient population.
5. **Reporting Results:** Report the results of the limit test accurately, including the method used, the limit calculation, and any relevant observations or comments.

3.3.1 Purpose and Principles of Limit Tests

Limit tests are analytical techniques used to determine the presence or absence of specified impurities or substances in pharmaceutical substances and dosage forms. These tests are designed to ensure that the levels of impurities or substances do not exceed predetermined limits set by regulatory authorities. The purpose of limit tests is to verify compliance with regulatory standards and specifications, ensuring the quality, safety, and efficacy of medicinal products.

Purpose of Limit Tests

1. **Compliance Verification:** Limit tests are used to verify compliance with regulatory standards and specifications, which specify the maximum allowable levels of impurities or substances in pharmaceutical products.
2. **Quality Assurance:** Limit tests help to ensure the quality of pharmaceutical products by detecting and quantifying impurities or substances at specified limits.
3. **Safety Assurance:** Limit tests contribute to the safety of pharmaceutical products by detecting harmful impurities or substances that may pose a risk to health.
4. **Stability Assessment:** Limit tests can be used to assess the stability of pharmaceutical products by monitoring the levels of impurities over time.

Principles of Limit Tests

1. **Specificity:** Limit tests should be specific for the impurity or substance being tested, ensuring that other components do not interfere with the test results.
2. **Sensitivity:** Limit tests should be sensitive enough to detect impurities or substances at or above the specified limits, even at low concentrations.
3. **Accuracy:** Limit tests should be accurate, providing results that are close to the true value of the impurity or substance being tested.
4. **Precision:** Limit tests should be precise, providing consistent results when repeated under the same conditions.
5. **Reproducibility:** Limit tests should be reproducible, providing similar results when performed by different analysts or in different laboratories.
6. **Robustness:** Limit tests should be robust, providing reliable results even when slight variations in experimental conditions occur.

3.3.2 Common Limit Tests

Limit tests are an essential part of pharmaceutical analysis, ensuring that pharmaceutical products meet the required quality standards. Several common limit tests are used to detect specific impurities or substances in pharmaceutical substances and dosage forms. These tests are designed to verify compliance with regulatory standards and specifications. This section provides an overview of some common limit tests used in pharmaceutical analysis.

3.3.2.1 Limit Test for Chlorides

The limit test for chlorides is a common analytical test used to detect the presence of chloride ions in pharmaceutical substances and dosage forms. Chloride ions can be present as impurities in raw materials or can result from the degradation of certain substances. The limit test for chlorides is based on the reaction between chloride ions and silver ions to form a white precipitate of silver chloride.

Principle: The principle of the limit test for chlorides is based on the reaction between chloride ions and silver ions in the presence of nitric acid. The reaction forms a white precipitate of silver chloride, which is insoluble in nitric acid.

Procedure: The procedure for the limit test for chlorides involves the following steps:

1. Preparation of Test Solution: Dissolve the sample in water or an appropriate solvent to obtain a test solution.
2. Addition of Nitric Acid: Add nitric acid to the test solution to acidify it and prevent the precipitation of other interfering ions.
3. Addition of Silver Nitrate Solution: Add silver nitrate solution to the test solution. The formation of a white precipitate indicates the presence of chloride ions.
4. Observation: Observe the formation of a white precipitate of silver chloride. The precipitate should be insoluble in nitric acid.

Interpretation: The presence of a white precipitate of silver chloride indicates the presence of chloride ions in the test sample. The intensity of the precipitate is proportional to the concentration of chloride ions in the sample.

The reaction involved in the limit test for chlorides can be represented by the following equation:

$$AgNO_3 + Cl^- \rightarrow AgCl + NO_3$$

In this reaction, silver nitrate ($AgNO_3$) reacts with chloride ions (Cl^-) to form silver chloride (AgCl) and nitrate ions ($NO3^-$) .The formation of a white precipitate of silver chloride confirms the presence of chloride ions in the test sample.

3.3.2.2 Limit Test for Sulphates

The limit test for sulphates is a common analytical test used to detect the presence of sulphate ions in pharmaceutical substances and dosage forms. Sulphate ions can be present as impurities in raw materials or can result from the degradation of certain substances. The limit test for sulphates is based on the precipitation reaction between sulphate ions and barium chloride, which forms a white precipitate of barium sulphate. This section provides an overview of the purpose, principles, procedure, and interpretation of the limit test for sulphates in pharmaceutical analysis.

Purpose and Principles

The purpose of the limit test for sulphates is to verify compliance with regulatory standards and specifications regarding the maximum allowable levels of sulphate ions in pharmaceutical products. The principle of the test is based on the reaction between sulphate ions and barium chloride in the presence of hydrochloric acid. The reaction forms a white precipitate of barium sulphate, which is insoluble in hydrochloric acid.

Procedure

The procedure for the limit test for sulphates involves the following steps:

1. Preparation of Test Solution: Dissolve the sample in water or an appropriate solvent to obtain a test solution.
2. Acidification: Add hydrochloric acid to the test solution to acidify it and prevent the precipitation of other interfering ions.
3. Addition of Barium Chloride Solution: Add barium chloride solution to the test solution. The formation of a white precipitate indicates the presence of sulphate ions.
4. Filtration: Filter the precipitate and wash it with water to remove any soluble impurities.
5. Drying and Weighing: Dry the precipitate and weigh it to determine the amount of sulphate ions present in the sample.

Interpretation

The presence of a white precipitate of barium sulphate indicates the presence of sulphate ions in the test sample. The intensity of the precipitate is proportional to the concentration of sulphate ions in the sample. The amount of sulphate ions can be quantified by measuring the weight of the precipitate and calculating the sulphate content based on the formula weight of barium sulphate.

The reaction involved in the limit test for sulphates can be represented by the following equation:

$BaCl2+SO4^{2-} \rightarrow BaSO_4+2Cl^-$

The formation of a white precipitate of barium sulphate confirms the presence of sulphate ions in the test sample.

3.3.2.3

Limit Test for Iron

Principle: This experiment involves comparing the purple color produced by the reaction of iron impurities with mercaptoacetic acid (thio glycollic acid) in the test sample to the standard color produced by a known quantity of iron under the same conditions. Citric acid (iron-free) is used to complex with metal cations other than iron, and mercaptoacetic acid also acts as a reducing agent, converting any Fe^{3+} present to Fe^{2+}. The purple color is due to the formation of ferrous mercaptoacetate in the presence of citric acid.

Formation of Ferrous Mercaptoacetate:

$Fe2++2HSCH2COOH+2H+ \rightarrow Fe(SCH2COOH)2+2H2O$

Reduction of Ferric to Ferrous Ion:

$Fe3++HSCH2COOH \rightarrow Fe2++HSCH2COO+H+$

Procedure:

1. **Test Solution:**

   - Dissolve the sample in 20 ml of water and transfer it to a Nessler cylinder.
   - Add 2 ml of 20% w/v iron-free citric acid and 0.1 ml of thioglycollic acid.
   - Make the solution alkaline with iron-free ammonia solution, dilute to 50 ml with water, and let it stand for 5 minutes.
   - Observe the color transversely.

2. Standard Solution:

- Transfer 2.0 ml of iron standard solution (20 ppm Fe) to a Nessler cylinder and dilute with 20 ml water.
- Add 2 ml of 20% w/v iron-free citric acid and 0.1 ml of thioglycollic acid.
- Make the solution alkaline with iron-free ammonia solution, dilute to 50 ml with water, and let it stand for 5 minutes.
- Observe the color transversely.

Observation: The test color should not be more intense than the standard color.

Preparation of Reagents:

- **0.05 M Sulphuric Acid:** Prepare solutions by adding 54x ml of sulphuric acid to an equal volume of water and diluting to 1000 ml with water.
- **20% w/v Iron-free Citric Acid:** Dissolve 20 g of iron-free citric acid in 100 ml water.
- **Iron-free Ammonia Solution:** Contains approximately 10% w/w of NH_3 (iron-free). Dilute 425 ml of strong ammonia solution to 1000 ml.
- **Iron Standard Solution (20 ppm Fe):** Dilute 1 volume of a 0.1726% w/v solution of ferric ammonium sulphate in 0.05 M sulphuric acid to 10 volumes with water. Contains iron in the ferric state.

Limit Test for Heavy Metals

Principle: The test involves comparing the color produced by the reaction of heavy metal impurities with a saturated solution of hydrogen sulfide to the standard color obtained by the reaction of a known quantity of lead with the same reagent.

Formation of Metal Sulfide:

$Pb2++H2S \rightarrow PbS\downarrow+2H+$

Removal of Hydrogen Sulfide Impurities:

$Pb(CH3COO)2+H2S \rightarrow PbS\downarrow+2CH3COOH$

Procedure:

1. Test Solution:

- ○ Dissolve the sample in 25 ml water and transfer it to a Nessler cylinder.
- ○ Adjust the pH to 3.0-4.0 with dilute acetic acid or dilute ammonia solution, dilute to 35 ml with water, and mix.
- ○ Add 10 ml of freshly prepared hydrogen sulfide solution, mix, dilute to 50 ml with water, and let it stand for 5 minutes.
- ○ View the color downward over a white surface.

2. **Standard Solution:**

- ○ Pipette 1.0 ml of lead standard solution (20 ppm Pb) into a Nessler cylinder and dilute with water to 25 ml.
- ○ Adjust the pH to 3.0-4.0 with dilute acetic acid or dilute ammonia solution, dilute to 35 ml with water, and mix.
- ○ Add 10 ml of freshly prepared hydrogen sulfide solution, mix, dilute to 50 ml with water, and let it stand for 5 minutes.
- ○ View the color downward over a white surface.

Methods:

- **Method I:** Used for substances giving a clear, colorless solution.
- **Method II:** Used for substances not giving a clear, colorless solution.
- **Method III:** Used for substances giving a clear, colorless solution in sodium hydroxide medium.

Observation: The test color should not be more intense than the standard color.

Preparation of Reagents:

- **Dilute Acetic Acid:** Contains approximately 6% w/w of CH_3 COOH. Dilute 57 ml of glacial acetic acid to 1000 ml with water.
- **Dilute Ammonia Solution:** Contains approximately 10% w/w of NH_3 . Dilute 425 ml of strong ammonia solution to 1000 ml. Store in well-closed containers in a cool place.
- **Lead Standard Solution (0.1% Pb):** Dissolve 0.400 g of lead nitrate in water containing 2 ml of nitric acid and add sufficient water to produce 250.0 ml.

- **Lead Standard Solution (100 ppm Pb):** Dilute 1 volume of lead standard solution (0.1% Pb) to 10 volumes with water.
- **Lead Standard Solution (20 ppm Pb):** Dilute 1 volume of lead standard solution (100 ppm Pb) to 5 volumes with water.

Limit Test for Arsenic

Principle: This test involves comparing the stain produced by arsenic impurities reacting with mercuric chloride paper (forming arsine gas) to the standard stain produced under the same conditions.

Conversion of Arsenic Acid to Arsine Gas:

$H_3AsO_4 \rightarrow H_3AsO_3$ $H_3AsO_3 + 3H_2 \rightarrow AsH_3\uparrow + 3H_2O$

Formation of Yellow Stain on Mercuric Chloride Paper:

$2AsH_3 + HgCl_2 \rightarrow Hg + 2HCl + As_2Hg_3$

Procedure:

Test Stain:

- Dissolve the sample in 50 ml water, add 10 ml of stannated hydrochloric acid, and transfer to the arsenic apparatus bottle.
- Add 5 ml of 1 M potassium iodide and 10 g of zinc AsT.
- Assemble the apparatus, immerse the bottle in a water bath to maintain uniform gas evolution, and observe the stain on the mercuric chloride paper after 40 minutes.

1. **Standard Stain:**

   - Transfer 1.0 ml of arsenic standard solution into the arsenic apparatus bottle and dilute to 50 ml with water.
   - Add 10 ml of stannated hydrochloric acid, 5 ml of 1 M potassium iodide, and 10 g of zinc AsT.
   - Assemble the apparatus, immerse the bottle in a water bath, and observe the stain on the mercuric chloride paper after 40 minutes.

Observation: The test stain should not be more intense than the standard stain.

Preparation of Reagents:

- **1 M Potassium Iodide:** Dissolve 166.0 g of potassium iodide in sufficient water to produce 1000 ml.
- **2 M Sodium Hydroxide:** Dissolve 40x of sodium hydroxide in sufficient water to produce 1000 ml.
- **Arsenic Standard Solution (10 ppm As):** Dissolve 0.330 g of arsenic trioxide in 5 ml of 2 M sodium hydroxide and dilute to 250.0 ml with water. Dilute 1 volume of this solution to 100 volumes with water.
- **Lead Acetate Cotton:** Immerse absorbent cotton in a mixture of 10 volumes of lead acetate solution and 1 volume of 2 M acetic acid. Drain excess liquid, allow to dry at room temperature, and store in tightly-closed containers.
- **Lead Acetate Paper:** Prepare from lead acetate solution, dry the impregnated paper at 100°C avoiding contact with metal.
- **Lead Acetate Solution:** A 10.0% w/v solution of lead acetate in carbon dioxide-free water.
- **Mercuric Chloride Paper:** Smooth white filter paper soaked in saturated mercuric chloride solution, dried at about 60°C in the dark.
- **Stannated Hydrochloric Acid:** Low in arsenic, commercial grade or prepared by adding 1 ml of stannous chloride solution to 100 ml of hydrochloric acid.
- **Stannous Chloride Solution:** Low in arsenic, commercially available or prepared from stannous chloride solution by adding an equal volume of hydrochloric acid, reducing to original volume by boiling, and filtering through fine-grain filter paper.

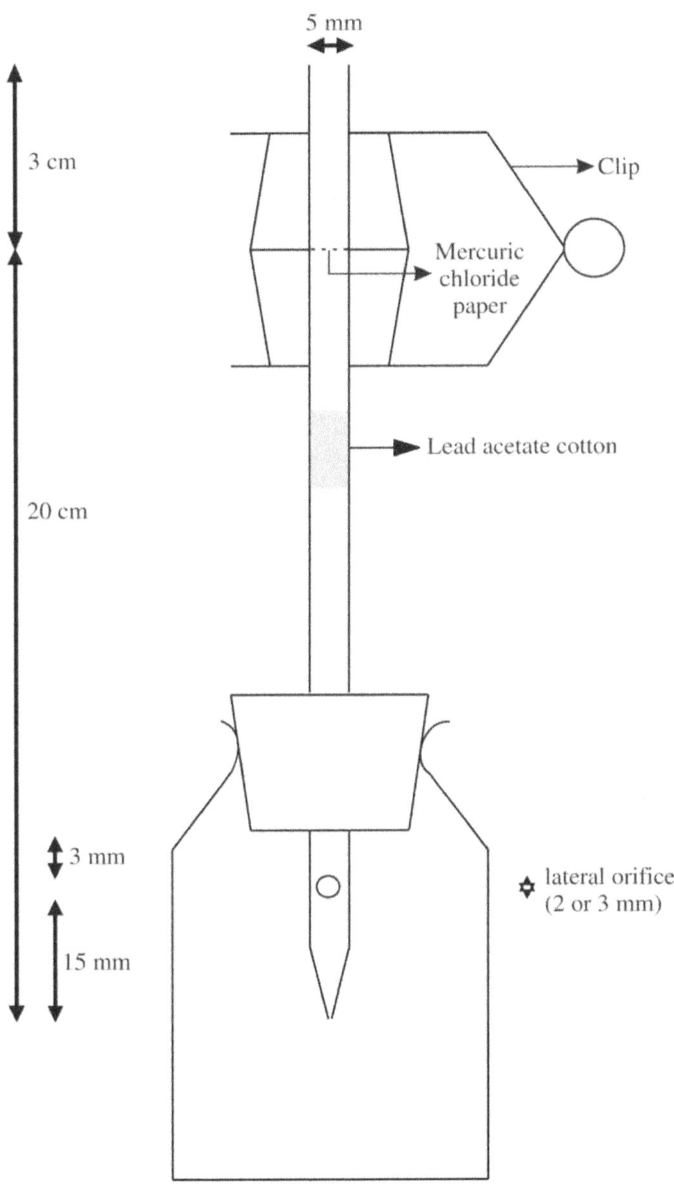

Arsenic Apparatus:

Limit Test for Lead

Principle: This test involves comparing the color produced in the chloroform layer by the reaction of lead impurities with diphenylthiocarbazone (dithizone) to the standard color produced under the same conditions. The dithizone in chloroform extracts lead from an alkaline aqueous solution as a lead-dithizone complex (violet in color).

Formation of Lead-Dithizone Complex:

$$Pb2++C6H5N2CSNHNH2 \rightarrow Pb(C6H5N2CSNHNH2)$$

Extraction and Complexation in Aqueous Solution: $Pb(C6H5N2CSNHNH2)2+HNO3 \rightarrow Pb(NO3)2+C6H5N2CSNHNH2$

Procedure:

1. **Test Solution:**

   - Dissolve the sample in water and transfer it to a separator.
   - Add 6 ml of ammonium citrate solution Sp. and 2 ml of hydroxylamine hydrochloride solution Sp.
   - Add two drops of phenol red solution and make the solution just alkaline with strong ammonia solution.
   - Cool the solution if necessary and add 2 ml of potassium cyanide solution Sp.
   - Extract the solution with several quantities of 5 ml dithizone extraction solution until the dithizone solution retains its green color.
   - Combine the dithizone solutions and shake with 30 ml of 1% v/v nitric acid for 30 seconds, then discard the chloroform layer.
   - Add 5 ml of dithizone standard solution to the acid solution and shake for 30 seconds. Observe the color of the chloroform layer.

2. **Standard Solution:**

   - Transfer a volume of lead standard solution (1 ppm Pb) equivalent to the amount of lead permitted in the substance being examined into a separator.
   - Add 6 ml of ammonium citrate solution Sp. and 2 ml of hydroxylamine hydrochloride solution Sp.
   - Add two drops of phenol red solution and make the solution just alkaline with strong ammonia solution.

- ○ Cool the solution if necessary and add 2 ml of potassium cyanide solution Sp.
- ○ Extract the solution with several quantities of 5 ml dithizone extraction solution until the dithizone solution retains its green color.
- ○ Combine the dithizone solutions and shake with 30 ml of 1% v/v nitric acid for 30 seconds, then discard the chloroform layer.
- ○ Add 5 ml of dithizone standard solution to the acid solution and shake for 30 seconds. Observe the color of the chloroform layer.

Observation: The test color of the chloroform layer should not be more intense than the standard color of the chloroform layer.

Preparation of Reagents:

- **1% v/v Nitric Acid:** Dilute 1 volume of nitric acid to 100 volumes with water.
- **Ammonium Citrate Solution Sp:** Dissolve 40 g of citric acid in 90 ml water, add 2 drops of phenol red solution, and add strong ammonia solution until the solution acquires a reddish color. Remove any lead by extracting with successive quantities of dithizone extraction solution until the dithizone solution retains its orange-green color.
- **Dithizone Extraction Solution:** Dissolve 30 mg of dithizone in 1000 ml of chloroform and add 5 ml of ethanol (95%). Store in a refrigerator.
- **Dithizone Standard Solution:** Dissolve 10 mg of dithizone in 1000 ml of chloroform. Store in a glass-stoppered lead-free, light-resistant bottle in a refrigerator.
- **Hydroxylamine Hydrochloride Solution Sp:** Dissolve 20 g of hydroxylamine hydrochloride in sufficient water to produce about 65 ml. Transfer to a separator, add 5 drops of thymol blue solution, and add strong ammonia solution until the solution becomes yellow. Add 10 ml of a 4% w/v solution of sodium diethyl dithiocarbamate, allow to stand for 5 minutes, and extract with successive quantities of chloroform until a 5 ml portion does not turn yellow when shaken with dilute cupric sulfate solution. Add dilute hydrochloric acid until the solution is pink, then add sufficient water to produce 100 ml.
- **Lead Standard Solution (0.1% Pb):** Dissolve 0.400 g of lead nitrate in water containing 2 ml of nitric acid and add sufficient water to produce 250.0 ml.

- **Lead Standard Solution (1 ppm Pb):** Dilute 1 volume of lead standard solution (10 ppm Pb) to 10 volumes with water.
- **Lead Standard Solution (10 ppm Pb):** Dilute 1 volume of lead standard solution (100 ppm Pb) to 10 volumes with water.
- **Lead Standard Solution (100 ppm Pb):** Dilute 1 volume of lead standard solution (0.1% Pb) to 10 volumes with water.
- **Potassium Cyanide Solution Sp:** Dissolve 50 g of potassium cyanide in sufficient water to produce 100 ml. Remove lead by extracting with successive quantities of dithizone extraction solution until the dithizone solution retains its orange-green color. Extract any dithizone remaining in the cyanide solution by shaking with chloroform. Dilute with sufficient water to produce a solution containing 10 g of potassium cyanide in each 100 ml.
- **Strong Ammonia Solution:** Contains 25.0% w/w NH_3 (limits 24.5 to 25.5); weight per ml about 0.91 g; strength about 13.5 M. Store in well-closed containers in a cool place.

CHAPTER IV

Acid–Base Titrations

Acid-Base Titrations in Pharmaceutical Analysis

Acid-base titrations are fundamental analytical techniques used to determine the concentration of an acid or a base in a sample. These titrations involve the reaction between an acid and a base, where one reacts with the other to form a neutral product. In pharmaceutical analysis, acid-base titrations are widely used to determine the concentration of active pharmaceutical ingredients (APIs) or to assess the acidity or alkalinity of pharmaceutical formulations. This section provides an overview of the purpose, principles, types, and applications of acid-base titrations in pharmaceutical analysis.

Purpose and Principles

The purpose of acid-base titrations in pharmaceutical analysis is to determine the concentration of acids or bases in a sample. The principle behind acid-base titrations is based on the concept of neutralization, where an acid reacts with a base to form a salt and water. The reaction is typically carried out in a controlled manner using a suitable indicator that changes color at the end point of the titration, indicating the completion of the reaction.

Types of Acid-Base Titrations

There are several types of acid-base titrations commonly used in pharmaceutical analysis, including:

1. **Strong Acid-Strong Base Titrations:** In these titrations, a strong acid is titrated against a strong base to determine the concentration of either the acid or the base.

2. **Weak Acid-Strong Base Titrations:** These titrations involve titrating a weak acid with a strong base to determine the concentration of the acid.

3. **Strong Acid-Weak Base Titrations:** In these titrations, a strong acid is titrated with a weak base to determine the concentration of the acid.

4. **Weak Acid-Weak Base Titrations:** These titrations involve titrating a weak acid with a weak base to determine the concentration of either the

acid or the base.

Procedure

The procedure for conducting an acid-base titration involves several key steps:

1. **Preparation of Solutions:** Prepare the acid and base solutions of known concentrations.
2. **Titration:** Add the base solution to the acid solution (or vice versa) using a burette until the equivalence point is reached.
3. **Indicator:** Add an indicator to the solution being titrated to signal the end point of the titration. Common indicators include phenolphthalein and methyl orange.
4. **Recording Results:** Record the volume of the base solution required to reach the end point of the titration.
5. **Calculations:** Use the volume and concentration of the base solution to calculate the concentration of the acid (or vice versa) in the sample.

Applications

Acid-base titrations are used in pharmaceutical analysis for various purposes, including:

1. **Determination of Drug Purity:** Acid-base titrations can be used to determine the purity of a drug substance by measuring the concentration of the active ingredient.
2. **Formulation Analysis:** Acid-base titrations can be used to assess the acidity or alkalinity of pharmaceutical formulations to ensure they meet regulatory standards.
3. **Quality Control:** Acid-base titrations are used in quality control processes to ensure the consistency and quality of pharmaceutical products.

4.1 Theories of Acid-Base Indicators

Acid-base indicators are substances that change color depending on the pH of the solution they are in. They are often used in acid-base titrations to determine the endpoint of the titration. The color change of an indicator is due to its ability to undergo a reversible chemical reaction. There are several theories that explain the behavior of acid-base indicators, including the Arrhenius theory, the Brønsted-Lowry theory, and the Lewis theory.

Arrhenius Theory: According to the Arrhenius theory, acids are substances that ionize in water to produce hydrogen ions (H^+), while bases are substances that ionize in water to produce hydroxide ions (OH^-) Acid-base indicators change color when the concentration of hydrogen ions or hydroxide ions in the solution changes. For example, phenolphthalein is colorless in acidic solutions but turns pink in basic solutions.

Brønsted-Lowry Theory: The Brønsted-Lowry theory defines acids as proton (hydrogen ion) donors and bases as proton acceptors. In this theory, acid-base indicators change color when they are either protonated or deprotonated. For example, methyl orange is red in acidic solutions (protonated form) and yellow in basic solutions (deprotonated form).

Lewis Theory: The Lewis theory defines acids as electron pair acceptors and bases as electron pair donors. According to this theory, acid-base indicators change color when they donate or accept an electron pair. For example, bromothymol blue is yellow in acidic solutions (accepts a proton, acts as a base) and blue in basic solutions (donates a proton, acts as an acid).

Application in Acid-Base Titrations: In acid-base titrations, indicators are chosen based on their color change at the endpoint of the titration. The choice of indicator depends on the pH range over which the titration is performed and the color change of the indicator in that pH range. Common indicators and their pH ranges include phenolphthalein (pH 8.3-10.0, colorless to pink), methyl orange (pH 3.1-4.4, red to yellow), and bromothymol blue (pH 6.0-7.6, yellow to blue).

4.1.1 Color Change Principles of Acid-Base Indicators

The color change exhibited by acid-base indicators is a fundamental aspect of their utility in titrations and pH determinations. This change in color is governed by several key principles, including the structure of the indicator molecule, its ionization state, and the pH of the solution. Understanding these principles is crucial for selecting the appropriate indicator for a specific titration or analytical procedure.

Indicator Molecule Structure: The structure of the indicator molecule plays a significant role in determining its color and color change properties. Indicators often contain conjugated systems of double bonds or aromatic rings, which can absorb light in the visible range. The presence of electron-donating or electron-withdrawing groups in the indicator molecule can also influence its color.

Ionization Equilibrium: In aqueous solutions, acid-base indicators exist in equilibrium between their acidic and basic forms. The ratio of the concentrations of these forms depends on the pH of the solution. At low pH (acidic conditions), indicators are predominantly in their acidic form, which may have one color. At high pH (basic conditions), indicators are predominantly in their basic form, which may have a different color. The transition from one color to another occurs over a narrow pH range, known as the indicator's pH range.

pH-Dependent Absorption Spectrum: The absorption spectrum of an indicator molecule is pH-dependent. This means that the wavelengths of light absorbed by the molecule change with the pH of the solution. As a result, the color of the indicator solution changes as the pH of the solution changes. For example, phenolphthalein is colorless in acidic solutions (pH < 8.3) but pink in basic solutions (pH > 10.0) due to a change in its absorption spectrum.

Color Change Mechanism: The color change of an indicator during a titration is a result of the change in the relative concentrations of its acidic and basic forms as the pH of the solution changes. Near the equivalence point of the titration, where the acid and base are present in nearly stoichiometric amounts, the pH of the solution changes rapidly, leading to a sharp change in the color of the indicator.

4.1.2 Selection of Indicators

The selection of an appropriate acid-base indicator is crucial in acid-base titrations to ensure accurate and reliable results. The choice of indicator depends on several factors, including the pH range of the titration, the color change of the indicator, and the nature of the titration (e.g., strong acid-strong base, weak acid-strong base). This section explores the principles behind the selection of acid-base indicators and provides guidelines for choosing the right indicator for a titration.

pH Range of the Titration: The pH range over which the titration occurs is a critical factor in selecting an indicator. The indicator's pH range should overlap with the pH range of the titration's equivalence point for optimal performance. For example, phenolphthalein is suitable for titrations with a pH range of 8.3-10.0, while methyl orange is suitable for titrations with a pH range of 3.1-4.4.

Color Change and Visibility: The color change of the indicator should be distinct and easily visible to the naked eye. The color change should occur rapidly and sharply around the equivalence point of the titration. Indicator solutions that are too dilute or have subtle color changes may lead to inaccurate endpoint determinations.

Nature of the Titration: The nature of the titration, such as whether it is a strong acid-strong base, weak acid-strong base, or other types of titrations, can influence the choice of indicator. Different indicators are more suitable for different types of titrations based on their pH ranges and color changes. For example, bromothymol blue is suitable for titrations involving weak acids and strong bases due to its pH range of 6.0-7.6.

Chemical Compatibility: The indicator should be chemically compatible with the substances being titrated and should not react with them to form insoluble precipitates or complexes that could interfere with the titration. For example, indicators containing sulfonic acid groups are often preferred over indicators containing carboxylic acid groups for titrations involving metal ions.

Sample Size and Volume: The volume of the sample being titrated and the volume of the titrant added can also influence the choice of indicator. For large sample volumes or small titrant volumes, indicators with a more pronounced color change may be preferred to ensure the endpoint is easily detected.

4.2 Classification of Acid-Base Titrations

Acid-base titrations are classified based on several factors, including the nature of the acid and base involved, the pH range of the titration, and the type of chemical reaction that occurs during the titration. Understanding the different types of acid-base titrations is essential for selecting the appropriate indicator and conducting the titration accurately. This section explores the classification of acid-base titrations and provides insights into each type.

1. Strong Acid-Strong Base Titrations: In strong acid-strong base titrations, a strong acid is titrated with a strong base. The reaction between the acid and base is rapid and complete, resulting in a neutralization reaction. The equivalence point of the titration occurs at a pH of 7, where the solution is neutral. Examples of strong acid-strong base titrations include the titration of hydrochloric acid (HCl) with sodium hydroxide (NaOH).

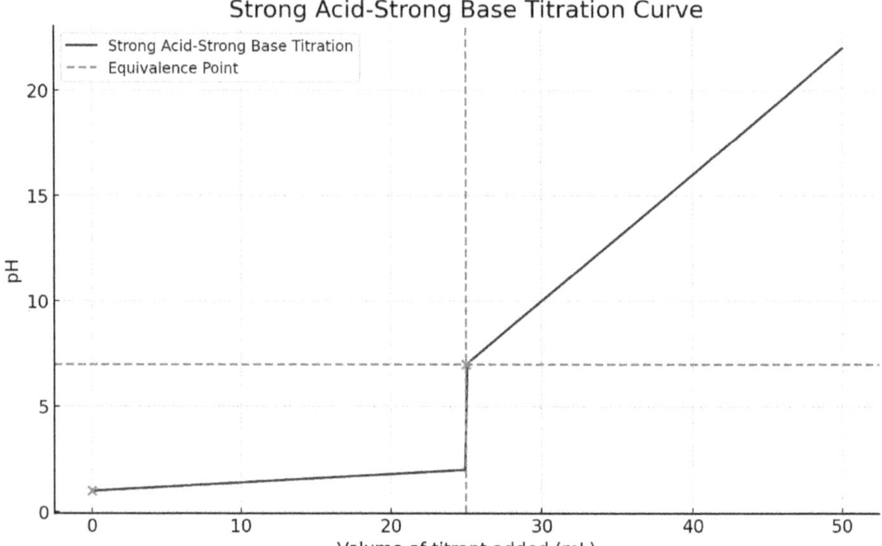

Strong acid-strong base titration curve. The initial pH is low (around 1-2), there is no significant buffer region, there is a sharp rise in pH around the equivalence point at pH 7, and the pH rises sharply after the equivalence point as excess strong base is added

2. Weak Acid-Strong Base Titrations: In weak acid-strong base titrations, a weak acid is titrated with a strong base. The pH at the equivalence point is greater than 7 due to the hydrolysis of the conjugate base of the weak acid. Common examples include the titration of acetic acid (CH_3COOH) with sodium hydroxide (NaOH).

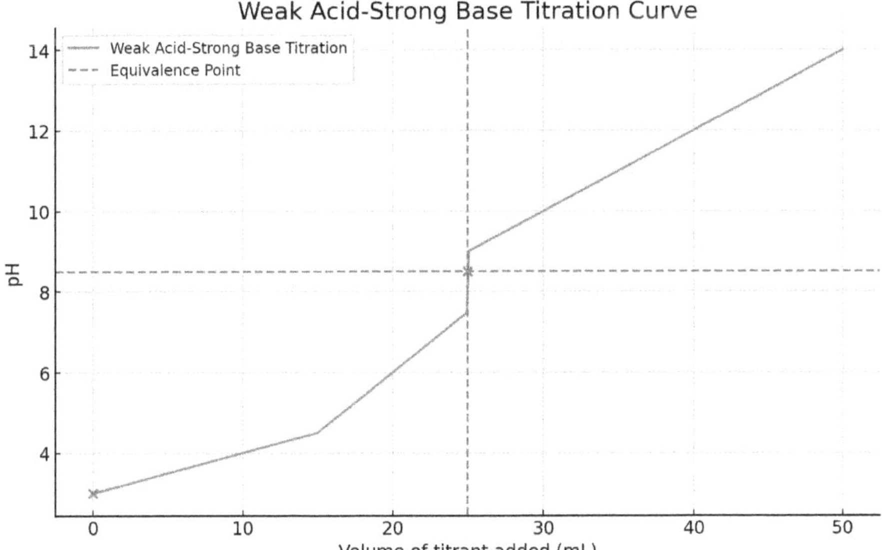

Weak acid-strong base titration curve. The initial pH is higher (around 3-4), there is a noticeable buffer region before the equivalence point, the equivalence point occurs above pH 7 (around 8.5), and the pH increases steadily after the equivalence point.

3. Strong Acid-Weak Base Titrations: In strong acid-weak base titrations, a strong acid is titrated with a weak base. The pH at the equivalence point is less than 7 due to the hydrolysis of the conjugate acid of the weak base. An example is the titration of hydrochloric acid (HCl) with ammonia (NH_3).

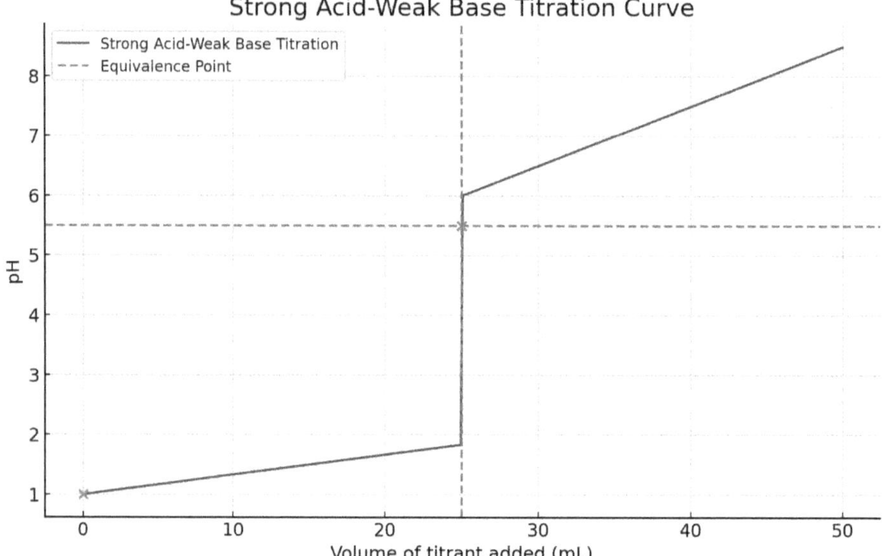

Strong acid-weak base titration curve. The initial pH is low (around 1-2), the equivalence point occurs below pH 7 (around 5.5), and the pH rises more gradually after the equivalence point as excess weak base is added.

4. Polyprotic Acid Titrations: Polyprotic acids have more than one ionizable hydrogen atom. The titration of a polyprotic acid involves multiple equivalence points, each corresponding to the deprotonation of one hydrogen atom. Phosphoric acid (H_3PO_4) is an example of a polyprotic acid that can be titrated with a strong base to form phosphates.

5. Titration of Mixtures: In some cases, mixtures of acids or bases may be titrated to determine their composition. The titration of a mixture of hydrochloric acid and acetic acid, for example, can be used to determine the concentration of each acid in the mixture.

6. Back Titration: In a back titration, an excess of a standard solution is added to the analyte, and the excess titrant is titrated with another standard solution. Back titrations are often used when the reaction between the analyte and titrant is slow or incomplete.

4.2.1 Strong Acids and Bases in Acid-Base Titrations

Strong acids and bases play a crucial role in acid-base titrations due to their complete ionization in aqueous solutions. This section explores the characteristics of strong acids and bases and their significance in acid-base titrations.

Characteristics of Strong Acids: Strong acids are acids that completely dissociate into their constituent ions in aqueous solutions. They have a low pKa value, indicating a strong tendency to donate protons. Examples of strong acids include hydrochloric acid (HCl), sulfuric acid ($H2SO_4$), and nitric acid (HNO_3).

Characteristics of Strong Bases: Strong bases are bases that completely dissociate into hydroxide ions (OH^-) in aqueous solutions. They have a high pKa value, indicating a strong tendency to accept protons. Examples of strong bases include sodium hydroxide (NaOH), potassium hydroxide (KOH), and calcium hydroxide (Ca(OH)2).

Significance in Acid-Base Titrations:

1. **Complete Ionization:** Strong acids and bases ionize completely in aqueous solutions, ensuring that the reaction goes to completion and allowing for precise titrations.
2. **Sharp Equivalence Point:** The complete ionization of strong acids and bases results in a sharp equivalence point in acid-base titrations. This sharp endpoint makes it easier to determine the volume of titrant required for neutralization.
3. **Standardization:** Strong acids and bases are often used to standardize solutions of unknown concentration. Their complete ionization ensures that the stoichiometry of the reaction is known, allowing for accurate determination of the concentration of the unknown solution.
4. **pH Range:** Strong acids and bases cover a wide pH range in aqueous solutions, making them suitable for a variety of titrations. For example, hydrochloric acid is suitable for titrations with a pH range of 1-7, while sodium hydroxide is suitable for titrations with a pH range of 7-14.

4.2.2 Weak Acids and Bases in Acid-Base Titrations

Weak acids and bases are compounds that only partially dissociate in aqueous solutions. Unlike strong acids and bases, which completely ionize, weak acids and bases establish an equilibrium between their ionized and non-ionized forms. This section discusses the characteristics of weak acids and bases and their role in acid-base titrations.

Characteristics of Weak Acids: Weak acids ionize partially in aqueous solutions, meaning that only a fraction of the acid molecules donate protons. They have a higher pKa value compared to strong acids, indicating a weaker tendency to donate protons. Examples of weak acids include acetic acid (CH_3COOH), citric acid ($C_6H_8O_7$), and carbonic acid ($H2CO_3$).

Characteristics of Weak Bases: Weak bases are compounds that only partially ionize in aqueous solutions to produce hydroxide ions (OH^-). They have a higher pKa value compared to strong bases, indicating a weaker tendency to accept protons. Examples of weak bases include ammonia (NH_3), methylamine (CH_3NH_2), and pyridine (C_5H_5N).

Role in Acid-Base Titrations:

1. **Equilibrium Reactions:** Weak acids and bases undergo equilibrium reactions in solution, leading to the formation of their conjugate bases or acids. This equilibrium affects the pH of the solution and the shape of the titration curve.

2. **Buffering Capacity:** Weak acids and bases have buffering capacity, meaning they can resist changes in pH upon addition of small amounts of acid or base. This property is utilized in buffer solutions used to calibrate pH meters and in biological systems to maintain pH stability.

3. **Titration Curve Shape:** The titration curve for a weak acid or base titration is different from that of a strong acid or base titration. It exhibits a gradual change in pH around the equivalence point due to the presence of the buffer region.

4. **Endpoint Detection:** The endpoint of a titration involving a weak acid or base is determined using a suitable indicator that changes color within the pH range of the buffer region. Common indicators for weak acid-base titrations include phenolphthalein and methyl orange.

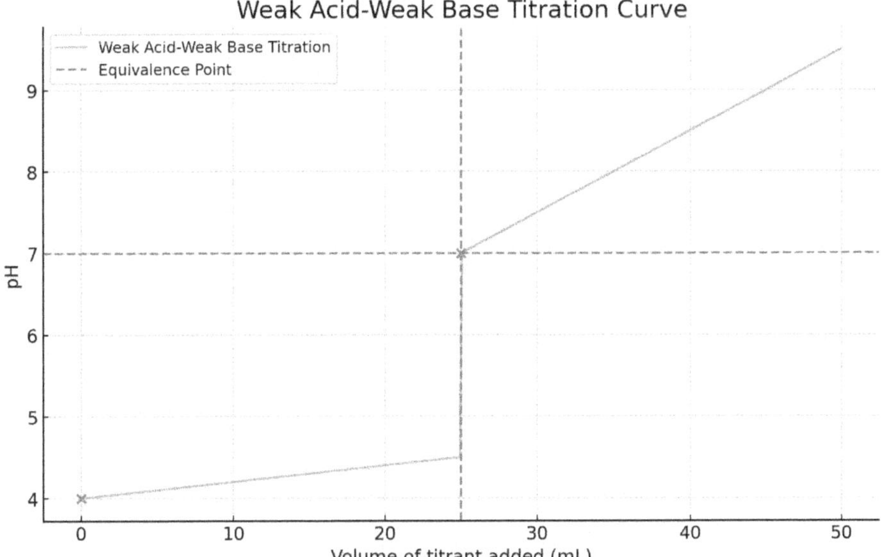

Weak acid-weak base titration curve. The initial pH is moderately low (around 4-5), the equivalence point is not well defined and occurs around pH 7 with a very gradual change, and the pH changes very gradually after the equivalence point.

4.2.3 Very Weak Acids and Bases in Acid-Base Titrations

Very weak acids and bases are compounds that exhibit extremely low ionization in aqueous solutions, leading to minimal concentration of ions in solution. Despite their limited ionization, these compounds can still participate in acid-base reactions, albeit to a lesser extent compared to weak acids and bases. This section explores the characteristics of very weak acids and bases and their relevance in acid-base titrations.

Characteristics of Very Weak Acids: Very weak acids have an extremely low tendency to donate protons in aqueous solutions, resulting in minimal ionization. Examples of very weak acids include boric acid (H_3BO_3) and hydrogen fluoride (HF).

Characteristics of Very Weak Bases: Very weak bases exhibit minimal ionization in aqueous solutions, leading to low concentrations of hydroxide ions (OH^-). Examples of very weak bases include ammonia (NH3) and water (H_2O).

Relevance in Acid-Base Titrations:

1. **pH Regulation:** Despite their low ionization, very weak acids and bases can contribute to the regulation of pH in solutions. Their presence can influence the overall pH of a solution, especially in dilute solutions or in the presence of other buffering agents.
2. **Equilibrium Considerations:** The ionization of very weak acids and bases follows equilibrium principles, with the equilibrium constant (Ka or Kb) reflecting the extent of ionization. These equilibrium constants are extremely small for very weak acids and bases, indicating their limited ionization.
3. **Titration Considerations:** In acid-base titrations involving very weak acids or bases, the titration curve exhibits gradual changes in pH around the equivalence point. The presence of these species can influence the shape of the titration curve and the selection of appropriate indicators.
4. **Analytical Considerations:** Despite their minimal ionization, very weak acids and bases can still be analyzed using titration techniques, although careful consideration must be given to factors such as the concentration of the species, the pH range of interest, and the sensitivity of the analytical method.

4.3 Neutralization Curves in Acid-Base Titrations

Neutralization curves, also known as titration curves, represent the change in pH of a solution as a strong acid is titrated with a strong base or vice versa. These curves provide valuable information about the progress of the titration and the equivalence point, where the acid and base have completely reacted. This section discusses the characteristics of neutralization curves and their significance in acid-base titrations.

Characteristics of Neutralization Curves:

1. **Shape:** Neutralization curves typically exhibit a characteristic shape, starting with a gradual increase in pH as the titrant is added, followed by a steep rise near the equivalence point, and ending with a gradual decrease in pH after the equivalence point.
2. **Equivalence Point:** The equivalence point is the point at which the acid and base have reacted completely, resulting in a solution that is

neither acidic nor basic. It is indicated by a sharp change in pH on the neutralization curve.

3. **Midpoint of the Curve:** The midpoint of the curve, also known as the half-equivalence point, corresponds to the point where half of the acid has reacted with the base. At this point, the pH of the solution is equal to the pKa of the acid being titrated.

4. **Slope of the Curve:** The slope of the curve is steepest at the equivalence point, indicating a rapid change in pH. Before and after the equivalence point, the slope is less steep, indicating a gradual change in pH.

5. **Buffer Regions:** Before and after the equivalence point, the curve may exhibit buffer regions where the pH remains relatively constant despite the addition of more titrant. These regions correspond to the presence of a weak acid and its conjugate base (or a weak base and its conjugate acid) in the solution.

Significance in Acid-Base Titrations:

1. **Endpoint Determination:** Neutralization curves help determine the endpoint of the titration, which is crucial for accurately determining the concentration of the analyte. The endpoint is often detected using a pH indicator that changes color at or near the equivalence point.

2. **Confirmation of Equivalence Point:** The equivalence point of the titration can be confirmed by identifying the point of inflection on the neutralization curve, which corresponds to the steepest slope and the highest rate of change in pH.

3. **Quantitative Analysis:** By analyzing the shape of the neutralization curve and the volume of titrant required to reach the equivalence point, one can calculate the concentration of the analyte with high precision.

4.3.2 Applications of Neutralization Curves in Analysis

Neutralization curves, generated during acid-base titrations, find widespread applications in analytical chemistry due to their ability to provide valuable information about the nature and concentration of analytes. This section explores the various applications of neutralization curves in quantitative and qualitative analysis.

Quantitative Analysis:

1. **Determination of Acid or Base Concentration:** Neutralization curves are used to determine the concentration of acids or bases in a sample by titrating them with a standard solution of known concentration. The volume of the standard solution required to reach the equivalence point is used to calculate the concentration of the analyte.
2. **Titration of Weak Acids and Bases:** Neutralization curves are particularly useful in titrations involving weak acids or bases. The gradual change in pH around the equivalence point allows for accurate determination of the endpoint, leading to precise calculations of the analyte's concentration.
3. **Titration of Mixtures:** Neutralization curves can be used to analyze mixtures of acids or bases by identifying multiple equivalence points corresponding to different components in the mixture. This allows for the determination of the concentrations of individual components.

Qualitative Analysis:

1. **Identification of Unknown Acids and Bases:** Neutralization curves can be used to identify unknown acids or bases by comparing their titration curves to those of known compounds. The shape and position of the equivalence point can provide clues about the identity of the unknown analyte.
2. **Detection of Impurities:** Neutralization curves can also be used to detect impurities in acids or bases. Impurities can alter the shape or position of the curve, indicating the presence of foreign substances in the sample.
3. **Buffer Capacity:** Neutralization curves can provide information about the buffer capacity of a solution. The presence of buffer regions on the curve indicates the ability of the solution to resist changes in pH upon addition of acid or base.

Environmental Analysis:

1. **Water Quality Analysis:** Neutralization curves can be used to analyze the pH of water samples, providing information about their acidity or alkalinity. This is important for assessing water quality and environmental impact.
2. **Soil Analysis:** Neutralization curves can also be used in soil analysis to determine the pH of soil samples. This information is crucial for

understanding soil fertility and its suitability for agriculture.

Neutralization curves play a crucial role in various analytical applications, including quantitative and qualitative analysis, environmental analysis, and industrial processes. By providing information about the nature and concentration of acids and bases, neutralization curves help analysts make informed decisions about chemical processes and environmental impact.

CHAPTER V

Non–Aqueous Titrations

5.1 Introduction to Non-Aqueous Titration

Non-aqueous titration is a titration technique where the titrant (the solution of known concentration) and the analyte (the solution of unknown concentration) are dissolved in solvents other than water. This section provides an overview of non-aqueous titration, its principles, and its applications in analytical chemistry.

Principles of Non-Aqueous Titration:

1. **Solvent Selection:** In non-aqueous titrations, solvents other than water, such as alcohols, acetic acid, and acetone, are used. The choice of solvent depends on the nature of the analyte and the titrant, as well as the solubility of the reaction products.
2. **Titration Techniques:** Non-aqueous titrations can be conducted using different techniques, including potentiometry, conductometry, and spectrophotometry. These techniques rely on the measurement of a physical property (such as voltage, conductivity, or absorbance) that changes as the titration progresses.
3. **Endpoint Detection:** The endpoint of a non-aqueous titration is typically detected using visual indicators or instrumental methods. Visual indicators change color when the reaction is complete, while instrumental methods measure a physical property that changes abruptly at the equivalence point.
4. **Applications:** Non-aqueous titration is commonly used in the analysis of pharmaceuticals, oils, fats, and other organic compounds. It is particularly useful for compounds that are insoluble or unstable in water.

Advantages of Non-Aqueous Titration:

1. **Increased Sensitivity:** Non-aqueous titrations often offer higher sensitivity compared to aqueous titrations, making them suitable for the analysis of trace amounts of analytes.

2. **Broad Applicability:** Non-aqueous titration can be used for a wide range of compounds, including weak acids and bases, as well as non-ionic compounds.

3. **Selective Reactions:** Some reactions occur more selectively in non-aqueous solvents, allowing for the determination of specific analytes in complex mixtures.

Limitations of Non-Aqueous Titration:

1. **Solubility Issues:** Some compounds may not be soluble in non-aqueous solvents, limiting the applicability of this technique.

2. **Reaction Specificity:** The selectivity of non-aqueous reactions can also be a limitation, as some reactions may not occur in non-aqueous solvents.

5.1.1 Importance and Applications of Non-Aqueous Titration

Non-aqueous titration plays a crucial role in analytical chemistry due to its versatility and applicability to a wide range of compounds. This section discusses the importance of non-aqueous titration and its various applications in pharmaceuticals, oils, and other industries.

Importance of Non-Aqueous Titration:

1. **Solubility Enhancement:** Non-aqueous solvents can dissolve a wider range of compounds compared to water, allowing for the analysis of substances that are insoluble in water.

2. **Increased Sensitivity:** Non-aqueous titration often offers higher sensitivity than aqueous titration methods, making it suitable for the analysis of trace amounts of substances.

3. **Selective Reactions:** Some reactions occur more selectively in non-aqueous solvents, allowing for the determination of specific analytes in complex mixtures.

Applications of Non-Aqueous Titration:

1. **Pharmaceutical Analysis:** Non-aqueous titration is widely used in pharmaceutical analysis to determine the purity and concentration of active pharmaceutical ingredients (APIs) in drug formulations. It is particularly useful for compounds that are insoluble or unstable in water.

2. **Oil and Fat Analysis:** Non-aqueous titration is used in the analysis of oils and fats to determine their acidity and iodine value. These parameters are important for quality control and product development in the food industry.

3. **Organic Compound Analysis:** Non-aqueous titration is used to analyze a wide range of organic compounds, including acids, bases, and non-ionic substances. It is particularly useful for compounds that are poorly soluble in water.

4. **Environmental Analysis:** Non-aqueous titration can be used in environmental analysis to determine the concentration of pollutants and contaminants in soil, water, and air samples. It is particularly useful for compounds that are not easily soluble in water.

5. **Industrial Applications:** Non-aqueous titration is used in various industries, including the chemical, pharmaceutical, and food industries, for quality control, process monitoring, and product development.

5.1.2 Types of Solvents Used in Non-Aqueous Titration

Non-aqueous titration involves the use of solvents other than water. The choice of solvent depends on the nature of the analyte and the titrant, as well as the solubility of the reaction products. This section explores the types of solvents commonly used in non-aqueous titration and their characteristics.

Common Solvents Used in Non-Aqueous Titration:

1. **Alcohols:** Alcohols such as methanol, ethanol, and isopropanol are commonly used as solvents in non-aqueous titrations. They are polar solvents that can dissolve a wide range of organic compounds.

2. **Acetic Acid:** Acetic acid is a weak acid that is often used as a solvent in non-aqueous titrations. It is particularly useful for titrations involving weak bases.

3. **Acetone:** Acetone is a polar aprotic solvent that is commonly used in non-aqueous titrations. It is particularly useful for titrations involving

ionic compounds.

4. **Dimethylformamide (DMF):** DMF is a polar solvent that is commonly used in non-aqueous titrations. It is particularly useful for titrations involving highly polar compounds.

5. **Dichloromethane:** Dichloromethane is a non-polar solvent that is commonly used in non-aqueous titrations. It is particularly useful for titrations involving non-polar compounds.

Factors to Consider When Choosing a Solvent:

1. **Solubility:** The solvent should be able to dissolve both the analyte and the titrant to ensure a complete reaction.

2. **Chemical Stability:** The solvent should be chemically stable and not react with the analyte or titrant.

3. **Non-Reactivity:** The solvent should not react with the analyte or titrant to avoid interference with the titration.

4. **Volatility:** The solvent should be volatile enough to be easily removed after the titration is complete.

5. **Safety:** The solvent should be safe to handle and not pose a risk to the operator or the environment.

5.2 Acidimetry and Alkalimetry in Non-Aqueous Titrations

Acidimetry and alkalimetry are titration techniques used to determine the concentration of acids and bases, respectively, in a sample. In non-aqueous titrations, these techniques are performed using solvents other than water. This section discusses the principles of acidimetry and alkalimetry in non-aqueous titrations and their applications in analytical chemistry.

Principles of Acidimetry and Alkalimetry:

1. **Acidimetry:** Acidimetry is the process of determining the concentration of an acid in a sample. It involves titrating the acid with a standard solution of base (alkali) until the equivalence point is reached. The endpoint is typically detected using a pH indicator or a potentiometric method.

2. **Alkalimetry:** Alkalimetry is the process of determining the concentration of a base (alkali) in a sample. It involves titrating the base with a standard solution of acid until the equivalence point is reached.

The endpoint is detected using a pH indicator or a potentiometric method.

Applications of Acidimetry and Alkalimetry in Non-Aqueous Titrations:

1. **Pharmaceutical Analysis:** Acidimetry and alkalimetry are widely used in pharmaceutical analysis to determine the acidity or alkalinity of drug formulations. This information is crucial for ensuring the stability and efficacy of the drugs.
2. **Food and Beverage Industry:** Acidimetry and alkalimetry are used in the food and beverage industry to determine the acidity or alkalinity of food products. This information is important for quality control and product development.
3. **Environmental Analysis:** Acidimetry and alkalimetry are used in environmental analysis to determine the acidity or alkalinity of soil and water samples. This information is important for assessing environmental impact and pollution levels.
4. **Industrial Applications:** Acidimetry and alkalimetry are used in various industries, including the chemical and textile industries, for quality control and process monitoring.

5.2.1 Principles and Techniques of Acidimetry and Alkalimetry in Non-Aqueous Titrations

Acidimetry and alkalimetry are fundamental titration methods used to determine the concentration of acids and bases, respectively, in a sample. In non-aqueous titrations, these techniques are applied using solvents other than water. This section delves into the principles and techniques of acidimetry and alkalimetry in non-aqueous titrations.

Principles of Acidimetry and Alkalimetry:

1. **Acidimetry:** Acidimetry involves the titration of an acidic solution with a standard solution of base (alkali) to determine the concentration of the acid. The reaction between the acid and base is typically a neutralization reaction, where the acid donates a proton (H+) to the base.
2. **Alkalimetry:** Alkalimetry involves the titration of a basic solution with a standard solution of acid to determine the concentration of the base. Similar to acidimetry, this process also involves a neutralization reaction,

where the base accepts a proton (H^+) from the acid.

Techniques of Acidimetry and Alkalimetry:

1. **Choice of Indicator:** Selecting a suitable indicator is crucial for accurately determining the endpoint of the titration. Common indicators used in non-aqueous titrations include phenolphthalein for alkalimetry and methyl orange for acidimetry.
2. **Endpoint Detection:** The endpoint of the titration is detected using visual indicators or instrumental methods. Visual indicators change color at the equivalence point, indicating the completion of the reaction. Instrumental methods, such as potentiometry, measure changes in voltage to determine the endpoint.
3. **Standardization of Solutions:** Before conducting the titration, both the acid and base solutions are standardized to ensure their accuracy. This is done by titrating the solutions with a primary standard solution of known concentration.
4. **Titration Procedure:** The titration is performed by adding the titrant (acid or base) to the analyte (acid or base) in a controlled manner until the endpoint is reached. The volume of titrant required to reach the endpoint is used to calculate the concentration of the analyte.

Applications of Acidimetry and Alkalimetry:

1. **Quality Control in Pharmaceuticals:** Acidimetry and alkalimetry are used to ensure the quality and purity of pharmaceutical products by determining the concentration of acids and bases in drug formulations.
2. **Environmental Analysis:** These titration techniques are employed in environmental analysis to assess the acidity or alkalinity of soil and water samples, aiding in environmental monitoring and pollution control.
3. **Food and Beverage Industry:** Acidimetry and alkalimetry are utilized in the food and beverage industry to determine the acidity or alkalinity of products, ensuring compliance with regulatory standards and quality control.

5.2.2 Examples and Case Studies in Acidimetry and Alkalimetry

Acidimetry and alkalimetry are essential analytical techniques used in various industries, including pharmaceuticals, food, and environmental monitoring. This section presents examples and case studies showcasing the practical applications of these techniques in non-aqueous titrations.

Example 1: Determination of Acidity in Pharmaceutical Formulations

Problem Statement: A pharmaceutical company needs to determine the acidity of a new drug formulation to ensure its stability and efficacy.

Methodology: Acidimetry is employed using a non-aqueous solvent such as ethanol. A sample of the drug formulation is titrated with a standard solution of sodium hydroxide (NaOH) using phenolphthalein as an indicator. The volume of NaOH required to reach the endpoint is recorded.

Results: The acidity of the drug formulation is determined based on the volume of NaOH used in the titration. This information helps the pharmaceutical company ensure that the formulation meets regulatory standards.

Example 2: Alkalimetry in Environmental Analysis

Problem Statement: A laboratory needs to determine the alkalinity of a water sample to assess its quality for environmental purposes.

Methodology: Alkalimetry is performed using a non-aqueous solvent such as acetone. The water sample is titrated with a standard solution of hydrochloric acid (HCl) using bromothymol blue as an indicator. The volume of HCl required to reach the endpoint is noted.

Results: The alkalinity of the water sample is determined based on the volume of HCl used in the titration. This information helps assess the water quality and its suitability for various purposes.

Case Study: Analysis of Citric Acid in Soft Drinks

Problem Statement: A beverage company wants to determine the citric acid content in its soft drinks for quality control purposes.

Methodology: Acidimetry is employed using a non-aqueous solvent such as methanol. A sample of the soft drink is titrated with a standard solution of sodium hydroxide (NaOH) using methyl orange as an indicator. The volume of NaOH required to reach the endpoint is recorded.

Results: The citric acid content in the soft drink is calculated based on the volume of NaOH used in the titration. This information helps the beverage company ensure that the citric acid content is within the specified range for the desired taste and quality of the soft drink.

5.3 Estimation Techniques in Non-Aqueous Titrations

Estimation techniques in non-aqueous titrations involve determining the concentration of a specific compound or functional group in a sample. This section explores the various estimation techniques used in non-aqueous titrations and their applications in analytical chemistry.

1. Precipitation Titration:

- **Principle:** Involves the formation of a precipitate through a titration reaction.
- **Application:** Used for the estimation of substances that form insoluble precipitates.

2. Complexometric Titration:

- **Principle:** Formation of a complex between the analyte and titrant.
- **Application:** Estimation of metal ions and compounds with specific functional groups.

3. Gravimetric Analysis:

- **Principle:** Based on the measurement of mass of a precipitate formed during a reaction.
- **Application:** Used for the estimation of substances that form stable and easily filterable precipitates.

4. Diazotization Titration:

- **Principle:** Formation of a diazonium salt from the analyte.
- **Application:** Estimation of compounds containing primary aromatic amines.

5. Redox Titration:

- **Principle:** Involves a redox reaction between the analyte and titrant.
- **Application:** Estimation of substances that can undergo oxidation-reduction reactions.

6. Conductometric Titration:

- **Principle:** Measurement of the change in conductivity during a titration.
- **Application:** Used for the estimation of substances that affect the conductivity of the solution.

7. Potentiometric Titration:

- **Principle:** Measurement of the change in potential during a titration.
- **Application:** Estimation of substances that can be detected by changes in electrode potential.

8. Spectrophotometric Titration:

- **Principle:** Measurement of absorbance or transmittance of light during a titration.
- **Application:** Estimation of substances that exhibit absorbance or transmittance properties.

5.3.1 Estimation of Sodium Benzoate

Sodium benzoate (NaC7H5O2) is a commonly used food preservative with the chemical formula NaC7H5O2. It is often used in acidic foods and beverages to inhibit the growth of bacteria, yeast, and mold. The estimation of sodium benzoate in non-aqueous titrations is important for quality control and regulatory compliance in the food industry.

Principle: The estimation of sodium benzoate can be carried out by titrating a solution containing sodium benzoate with a standard solution of a strong base, such as sodium hydroxide (NaOH), using a suitable indicator.

Procedure:

1. **Preparation of Sample:** A known volume of the sample containing sodium benzoate is taken and diluted to a suitable volume with a non-aqueous solvent, such as ethanol or acetone.
2. **Titration:** The sample solution is titrated with a standard solution of sodium hydroxide (NaOH) using a suitable indicator, such as phenolphthalein. The titration is performed until the endpoint is reached, indicated by a color change of the indicator.
3. **Calculation:** The concentration of sodium benzoate in the sample can be calculated using the volume and concentration of the NaOH solution used in the titration.

Example Calculation: If 25.0 mL of a sample containing sodium benzoate is titrated with 0.100 M NaOH solution and 20.0 mL of NaOH solution is required to reach the endpoint, the concentration of sodium benzoate in the sample can be calculated as follows:

Concentration of NaOH×Volume of NaOH=Concentration of $NaC_7H_5O_2$×Volume of Sample

0.100 M×20.0 mL=Concentration of NaC7H5O2×25.0 mL Concentration of $NaC_7H_5O_2$=0.100 M×20.0 mL / 25.0 mL Concentration of NaC7H5O2=0.080 M

5.3.2 Estimation of Ephedrine Hydrochloride (Ephedrine HCl)

Ephedrine hydrochloride (C10H15NO.HCl) is a salt of ephedrine, a sympathomimetic amine commonly used as a decongestant and bronchodilator. The estimation of ephedrine HCl in non-aqueous titrations is important for pharmaceutical analysis and quality control.

Principle: The estimation of ephedrine HCl can be carried out by titrating a solution containing ephedrine HCl with a standard solution of a strong acid, such as hydrochloric acid (HCl), using a suitable indicator.

Procedure:

1. **Preparation of Sample:** A known volume of the sample containing ephedrine HCl is taken and dissolved in a non-aqueous solvent, such as ethanol or methanol.
2. **Titration:** The sample solution is titrated with a standard solution of hydrochloric acid (HCl) using a suitable indicator, such as bromothymol blue. The titration is performed until the endpoint is reached, indicated by a color change of the indicator.
3. **Calculation:** The concentration of ephedrine HCl in the sample can be calculated using the volume and concentration of the HCl solution used in the titration.

Example Calculation: If 10.0 mL of a sample containing ephedrine HCl is titrated with 0.100 M HCl solution and 15.0 mL of HCl solution is required to reach the endpoint, the concentration of ephedrine HCl in the sample can be calculated as follows:

Concentration of HCl×Volume of HCl=Concentration of Ephedrine HCl×Volume of Sample

0.100 M×15.0 mL=Concentration of Ephedrine HCl×10.0 mL Concentration of Ephedrine HCl=0.100 M×15.0 mL/100mL

Concentration of Ephedrine HCl=0.150M

The estimation of ephedrine HCl in non-aqueous titrations is a valuable technique for determining the concentration of this important pharmaceutical compound. By following the appropriate procedures and calculations, analysts can ensure the quality and efficacy of pharmaceutical products containing ephedrine HCl.

CHAPTER VI

Precipitation and Complexometric Titrations

6.1 Precipitation Titrations

Precipitation titrations are a type of volumetric analysis that involves the formation of a precipitate as the endpoint of the titration. This method is particularly useful for the determination of halides, sulfates, and many organic substances. The principle behind precipitation titrations is based on the reaction between the analyte and a standard titrant to form an insoluble precipitate. The endpoint of the titration is reached when the precipitate is formed in the solution, indicating the completion of the reaction.

Principle of Precipitation Titrations: In precipitation titrations, a precipitating agent is added to the solution containing the analyte. The precipitating agent reacts with the analyte to form a precipitate. The endpoint of the titration is reached when all the analyte has reacted with the precipitating agent, and no further precipitate forms. The formation of the precipitate is often indicated by a visual change, such as the appearance of turbidity or a color change.

Types of Precipitation Titrations:

1. **Mohr's Method:** This method is used for the titration of halides (chlorides, bromides, and iodides) with a silver nitrate ($AgNO_3$) solution in the presence of a chromate indicator.
2. **Volhard Method:** This method is used for the titration of halides with a standard solution of silver nitrate ($AgNO_3$) in the presence of a potassium chromate indicator.
3. **Fajans Method:** This method is used for the titration of halides with a standard solution of silver nitrate ($AgNO_3$) using a adsorption indicator such as ferric ammonium sulfate.
4. **Modified Volhard Method:** This method is similar to the Volhard method but uses a back titration with a standard solution of ammonium thiocyanate (NH_4SCN) in the presence of iron (III) as an indicator.

Applications of Precipitation Titrations: Precipitation titrations are widely used in various industries and laboratories for the determination of various substances. Some common applications include:

- Determination of chloride, bromide, and iodide ions in water samples.
- Analysis of pharmaceuticals containing halides.
- Determination of sulfate ions in fertilizers and industrial products.
- Analysis of organic substances such as proteins and nucleic acids.

6.1.1 Mohr's Method

Mohr's method is a classic technique used in precipitation titrations for the determination of halides, particularly chloride ions (Cl^-). This method relies on the formation of a silver chloride (AgCl) precipitate, which is insoluble in water and appears as a white precipitate. The endpoint of the titration is detected by the formation of this precipitate, which is visually observed as the appearance of a turbidity in the solution.

Principle: In Mohr's method, a known volume of the sample containing chloride ions is titrated with a standard solution of silver nitrate (AgNO3) using a chromate indicator, typically potassium chromate (K2CrO4). The silver ions (Ag^+) from the silver nitrate react with the chloride ions (Cl^-) in the sample to form a white precipitate of silver chloride (AgCl):

$$Ag^+ + Cl^- \rightarrow AgCl$$

The endpoint of the titration is reached when all the chloride ions in the sample have reacted with the silver ions, and no more silver chloride precipitate forms. At this point, the appearance of a reddish-brown color due to the formation of silver chromate (Ag2CrO4) indicates the endpoint.

Procedure:

1. Prepare a standard solution of silver nitrate (AgNO3) and add a few drops of potassium chromate indicator to it.
2. Titrate the sample containing chloride ions with the standard silver nitrate solution until the appearance of a reddish-brown color, indicating the endpoint.
3. Note the volume of silver nitrate solution required to reach the endpoint and calculate the concentration of chloride ions in the sample.

Applications: Mohr's method is commonly used in the analysis of chloride ions in various samples, including drinking water, wastewater, and food products. It is a simple and reliable method for the determination of chloride content and is widely used in analytical chemistry laboratories.

Limitations: One of the limitations of Mohr's method is the formation of a colored endpoint with the chromate indicator, which can make it difficult to detect the exact endpoint. Additionally, other ions such as bromide and iodide can interfere with the titration and affect the accuracy of the results.

6.1.2 Volhard's Method

Volhard's method is a titration technique used for the determination of halide ions, particularly chloride ions (Cl^-), in a solution. This method is based on the titration of the excess silver ions ($Ag+$) after the chloride ions have been precipitated with a known excess of silver nitrate ($AgNO3$) solution. The endpoint of the titration is detected by the appearance of a reddish-brown color due to the formation of silver chromate ($Ag2CrO4$) precipitate.

Principle: In Volhard's method, a known volume of the sample containing chloride ions is titrated with a standard solution of silver nitrate ($AgNO3$) in the presence of a potassium chromate ($K2CrO4$) indicator. The chloride ions in the sample react with the silver ions to form a white precipitate of silver chloride ($AgCl$):

$$Ag^{+}+Cl^{-}\rightarrow AgCl$$

After all the chloride ions have reacted, any excess silver ions react with the chromate ions to form silver chromate:

$$Ag^{+}+2CrO4^{2-}\rightarrow Ag_2CrO4$$

The appearance of a reddish-brown color indicates the endpoint of the titration.

Procedure:

1. Prepare a standard solution of silver nitrate ($AgNO3$) and add a few drops of potassium chromate indicator to it.
2. Titrate the sample containing chloride ions with the standard silver nitrate solution until the appearance of a reddish-brown color, indicating the endpoint.
3. Note the volume of silver nitrate solution required to reach the endpoint and calculate the concentration of chloride ions in the sample.

Applications: Volhard's method is commonly used in the analysis of chloride ions in various samples, including food products, environmental samples, and pharmaceuticals. It is a reliable method for the determination of chloride content and is widely used in analytical chemistry laboratories.

Limitations: One limitation of Volhard's method is the formation of a colored endpoint with the chromate indicator, which can make it difficult to detect the exact endpoint. Additionally, the presence of other ions such as bromide and iodide can interfere with the titration and affect the accuracy of the results.

6.1.3 Modified Volhard's Method

Modified Volhard's method is a variation of the classic Volhard method used for the determination of halide ions, particularly chloride ions (Cl^-). This method is based on the back titration of the excess silver ions ($Ag+$) after the chloride ions have been precipitated with a known excess of silver nitrate ($AgNO3$) solution. The endpoint of the titration is detected by the appearance of a reddish-brown color due to the formation of silver chromate ($Ag2CrO4$) precipitate.

Principle: In the Modified Volhard's method, a known volume of the sample containing chloride ions is titrated with a standard solution of silver nitrate ($AgNO3$) in the presence of a potassium chromate ($K2CrO4$) indicator. The chloride ions in the sample react with the silver ions to form a white precipitate of silver chloride ($AgCl$):

$$Ag^+ + Cl^- \rightarrow AgCl$$

After all the chloride ions have reacted, any excess silver ions react with the chromate ions to form silver chromate:

$$Ag+ + 2CrO_4{}^{2-} \rightarrow Ag_2CrO_4$$

The appearance of a reddish-brown color indicates the endpoint of the titration.

Procedure:

1. Prepare a standard solution of silver nitrate ($AgNO3$) and add a few drops of potassium chromate indicator to it.
2. Titrate the sample containing chloride ions with the standard silver nitrate solution until the appearance of a reddish-brown color, indicating the endpoint.
3. Note the volume of silver nitrate solution required to reach the endpoint.

4. Add a few drops of iron (III) nitrate solution to the titrated solution to mask the excess silver ions.
5. Back titrate the remaining silver ions with a standard solution of ammonium thiocyanate (NH4SCN) until the appearance of a reddish-brown color, indicating the endpoint.
6. Note the volume of ammonium thiocyanate solution required to reach the endpoint.

Applications: Modified Volhard's method is commonly used in the analysis of chloride ions in various samples, including food products, environmental samples, and pharmaceuticals. It is a reliable method for the determination of chloride content and is widely used in analytical chemistry laboratories.

Limitations: One limitation of Modified Volhard's method is the formation of a colored endpoint with the chromate indicator, which can make it difficult to detect the exact endpoint. Additionally, the presence of other ions such as bromide and iodide can interfere with the titration and affect the accuracy of the results.

6.1.4 Fajans Method

The Fajans method is a titration technique used for the determination of halide ions, particularly chloride ions (Cl^-), in a solution. This method is based on the adsorption of a colored indicator on the precipitate surface formed during the titration. The endpoint of the titration is detected by the formation of an adsorption complex, which results in a color change in the solution.

Principle: In the Fajans method, a known volume of the sample containing chloride ions is titrated with a standard solution of silver nitrate ($AgNO_3$) in the presence of an adsorption indicator, typically ferric ammonium sulfate. The chloride ions in the sample react with the silver ions to form a white precipitate of silver chloride ($AgCl$):

$$Ag^+ + Cl^- \rightarrow AgCl$$

As the titration progresses, the adsorption indicator is added, which forms an adsorption complex with the silver ions on the surface of the precipitate. This complex formation results in a color change in the solution, indicating the endpoint of the titration.

Procedure:

1. Prepare a standard solution of silver nitrate (AgNO3).
2. Add a few drops of an adsorption indicator (e.g., ferric ammonium sulfate) to the silver nitrate solution.
3. Titrate the sample containing chloride ions with the standard silver nitrate solution until the appearance of a color change, indicating the endpoint.
4. Note the volume of silver nitrate solution required to reach the endpoint and calculate the concentration of chloride ions in the sample.

Applications: The Fajans method is commonly used in the analysis of chloride ions in various samples, including water, food products, and pharmaceuticals. It is a sensitive method for the determination of chloride content and is widely used in analytical chemistry laboratories.

Limitations: One limitation of the Fajans method is the need for a suitable adsorption indicator, which can be specific to certain ions and may not be suitable for all samples. Additionally, the presence of other ions such as bromide and iodide can interfere with the titration and affect the accuracy of the results.

6.2 Estimation of Sodium Chloride

Sodium chloride (NaCl), commonly known as table salt, is a vital compound with numerous applications in the food industry, medicine, and chemical manufacturing. Its estimation is crucial in various fields to ensure product quality and safety. Several methods are available for the estimation of sodium chloride, including gravimetric, titrimetric, and instrumental techniques.

Gravimetric Method: The gravimetric method for estimating sodium chloride involves the precipitation of chloride ions as silver chloride (AgCl) and subsequent weighing of the precipitate. This method is based on the reaction between chloride ions and silver ions from silver nitrate (AgNO3) solution:

NaCl+AgNO3→AgCl+NaNO3

The silver chloride precipitate is filtered, washed, dried, and weighed to determine the chloride content in the sample.

Titrimetric Methods:

1. **Mohr's Method:** In Mohr's method, chloride ions in the sample are titrated with a standard silver nitrate (AgNO3) solution in the presence of a chromate indicator. The endpoint is detected by the formation of a

red precipitate of silver chromate (Ag2CrO4).

2. **Volhard Method:** The Volhard method involves the titration of excess silver ions with a standard solution of ammonium thiocyanate (NH4SCN) in the presence of ferric ammonium sulfate indicator after the chloride ions have been precipitated with silver nitrate.

Instrumental Methods:

1. **Ion-Selective Electrode (ISE):** ISE is a fast and accurate method for the estimation of chloride ions in a sample. It involves the use of a chloride-selective electrode that measures the potential difference between the electrode and the sample solution.
2. **Conductometric Method:** The conductometric method relies on the change in conductivity of a solution upon the addition of silver nitrate. The endpoint is detected by a sudden increase in conductivity due to the formation of insoluble silver chloride.

6.2.1 Procedure and Calculations for Estimation of Sodium Chloride Gravimetric Method:

1. Weigh a clean, dry, and pre-ignited crucible accurately.
2. Pipette a known volume of the sample solution into the crucible.
3. Add a few drops of nitric acid to the solution to prevent the precipitation of other metal ions.
4. Add a few drops of silver nitrate solution to precipitate chloride ions as silver chloride.
5. Heat the crucible gently to evaporate the solution and then heat strongly to decompose any excess nitrate.
6. Cool and weigh the crucible with the silver chloride precipitate.
7. Calculate the percentage of chloride ions in the sample using the formula:

%NaCl= (WAgCl / Wsample)×100
where:

- WAgCl = weight of silver chloride precipitate
- Wsample= weight of the sample used

Titrimetric Methods:

1. **Mohr's Method:**

   - Titrate the chloride ions in the sample with a standard silver nitrate solution until the formation of a red precipitate of silver chromate.
   - Calculate the concentration of chloride ions in the sample using the formula:

   Chloride ion concentration=VAgNO3×NAgNO3×35.45 / Vsample
   where:

   - VAgNO3 = volume of silver nitrate solution used
   - NAgNO3 = normality of the silver nitrate solution
   - Vsample = volume of the sample used

2. **Volhard Method:**

   - Titrate the excess silver ions with a standard ammonium thiocyanate solution until the formation of a reddish-brown color.
   - Calculate the chloride ion concentration using the formula:

   Chloride ion concentration=VNH4SCN×NNH4SCN×35.45
   where:

   - VNH4SCN= volume of ammonium thiocyanate solution used
   - NNH4SCNN
   - Vsample = volume of the sample used

6.2.2 Applications of Sodium Chloride Estimation in Pharmaceutical Analysis

Sodium chloride plays a crucial role in pharmaceutical formulations, and its accurate estimation is essential to ensure product quality, efficacy, and safety. The estimation of sodium chloride in pharmaceutical analysis finds applications in various areas:

1. Parenteral Solutions: Sodium chloride is commonly used as a diluent or isotonic agent in parenteral solutions. Its concentration must be accurately controlled to maintain isotonicity, which is critical for the compatibility and stability of the formulation.

2. Ophthalmic Solutions: Sodium chloride is used in ophthalmic solutions to adjust tonicity and ensure compatibility with ocular tissues. Accurate estimation is essential to prevent irritation or damage to the eyes.

3. Intravenous Fluids: Sodium chloride is a component of intravenous fluids used for hydration and electrolyte balance. Estimating its concentration ensures the proper formulation of these fluids for therapeutic use.

4. Hemodialysis Solutions: Sodium chloride is used in hemodialysis solutions to maintain electrolyte balance during the procedure. Accurate estimation is crucial to prevent electrolyte imbalances in patients undergoing hemodialysis.

5. Pharmaceutical Excipients: Sodium chloride is used as an excipient in tablet formulations to improve tablet hardness and disintegration. Estimation ensures the correct amount of sodium chloride is used to achieve the desired tablet properties.

6. Inhalation Solutions: Sodium chloride solutions are used in inhalation therapies for respiratory conditions. Accurate estimation is important to ensure the correct concentration for effective treatment.

7. Stability Studies: Estimation of sodium chloride is essential in stability studies of pharmaceutical formulations to monitor changes in concentration over time, which can affect product quality and shelf-life.

8. Quality Control: Sodium chloride estimation is part of quality control measures to ensure pharmaceutical products meet regulatory standards for purity, potency, and safety.

Conclusion: Accurate estimation of sodium chloride in pharmaceutical analysis is critical for ensuring the quality, safety, and efficacy of pharmaceutical products. Various analytical methods, including gravimetric and titrimetric techniques, are employed for this purpose, depending on the specific requirements of the analysis.

6.3 Complexometric Titrations

Complexometric titrations are a type of volumetric analysis used to determine the concentration of metal ions in a solution. These titrations rely on the formation of stable complexes between metal ions and complexing agents (ligands). The endpoint of the titration is determined by the formation of a colored complex or by using a metal ion indicator.

Introduction: Complexometric titrations are widely used in analytical chemistry for the determination of metal ions due to their high specificity and sensitivity. The most commonly used complexing agent is ethylenediaminetetraacetic acid (EDTA), which forms stable complexes with a wide range of metal ions.

Procedure:

1. Prepare a solution containing the metal ion to be determined.
2. Add a few drops of an appropriate indicator or use a pH meter to monitor the reaction.
3. Titrate the metal ion solution with a standard solution of the complexing agent (e.g., EDTA) until the formation of a colored complex or a sharp change in pH.
4. Note the volume of the standard solution required to reach the endpoint.
5. Calculate the concentration of the metal ion in the sample using the stoichiometry of the reaction.

Example Reaction: The titration of calcium ions (Ca^{2+}) with EDTA can be represented as follows:

$$Ca^{2+} + EDTA^{4-} \rightarrow Ca(EDTA)2^{-}$$

Applications: Complexometric titrations are used in various industries and research fields for the determination of metal ions. Some common applications include:

- Determination of calcium and magnesium ions in water samples.
- Determination of zinc, copper, and iron ions in pharmaceutical formulations.
- Analysis of trace metal ions in biological samples.
- Quality control of food and beverages for metal ion content.

6.3.1 Classification and Techniques of Complexometric Titrations

Complexometric titrations are classified based on the nature of the complexing agent and the metal ion being titrated. These titrations employ different techniques to achieve accurate and precise results. The classification and techniques of complexometric titrations are as follows:

Classification:

1. **Direct Titration:** In direct titrations, the complexing agent is added directly to the solution containing the metal ion until the endpoint is reached.
2. **Back Titration:** In back titrations, an excess of the complexing agent is added to the solution containing the metal ion. Then, the unreacted complexing agent is titrated with a standard solution of another metal ion to determine the amount of excess complexing agent.

Techniques:

1. **EDTA Titration:** Ethylenediaminetetraacetic acid (EDTA) is the most commonly used complexing agent in complexometric titrations. It forms stable complexes with a wide range of metal ions.
2. **Masking:** Masking agents are used to prevent interference from other ions present in the sample. These agents form complexes with interfering ions, preventing them from reacting with the complexing agent.
3. **Selective Complexation:** Selective complexation involves the use of complexing agents that selectively form complexes with specific metal ions. This technique is used to determine individual metal ions in a mixture.
4. **Buffering:** Buffer solutions are used to maintain a constant pH during the titration, which is crucial for the formation of stable complexes.
5. **Indicator Selection:** Indicators are used to detect the endpoint of the titration. Metal ion indicators, such as Eriochrome Black T, are commonly used in complexometric titrations.

Applications: Complexometric titrations find applications in various fields, including:

- Environmental analysis: Determination of metal ions in water and soil samples.
- Pharmaceutical analysis: Analysis of metal ions in pharmaceutical formulations.
- Industrial analysis: Quality control of metal ions in industrial processes.
- Biological analysis: Determination of metal ions in biological samples.

6.3.2 Metal Ion Indicators in Complexometric Titrations

Metal ion indicators are essential components of complexometric titrations, used to detect the endpoint of the titration. These indicators form complexes with metal ions, leading to color changes that signal the completion of the titration. The selection of a suitable metal ion indicator depends on the specific metal ion being titrated and the pH of the solution.

Types of Metal Ion Indicators:

1. **Eriochrome Black T (EBT):** EBT is a commonly used indicator in complexometric titrations. It forms wine-red complexes with metal ions in the presence of EDTA. The color change from wine-red to blue signals the endpoint of the titration.
2. **Calcein:** Calcein is another indicator used for the titration of calcium ions. It forms a fluorescent complex with calcium ions, which can be detected using fluorescence spectroscopy.
3. **Murexide:** Murexide is used for the titration of calcium and magnesium ions. It forms a red-violet complex with these ions, and the color change indicates the endpoint of the titration.
4. **Xylenol Orange:** Xylenol Orange is used for the titration of aluminum and beryllium ions. It forms a red complex with these ions, and the color change to yellow signals the endpoint.
5. **Calmagite:** Calmagite is used for the titration of magnesium ions. It forms a red-violet complex with magnesium ions, and the color change to blue signals the endpoint.

Selection Criteria for Metal Ion Indicators:

- The indicator should form a stable complex with the metal ion being titrated.
- The color change should be sharp and distinct to indicate the endpoint accurately.
- The indicator should not interfere with the complexation reaction between the metal ion and the complexing agent.

Applications of Metal Ion Indicators: Metal ion indicators are widely used in various industries and research fields for the determination of metal ions in samples. They are particularly useful in environmental analysis, pharmaceutical analysis, and industrial quality control.

6.3.3 Masking and Demasking Reagents in Complexometric Titrations

Masking and demasking reagents are used in complexometric titrations to prevent interference from other ions in the sample or to selectively release a metal ion from a complex. These reagents play a crucial role in ensuring the accuracy and specificity of the titration.

Masking Reagents:

- Masking reagents form stable complexes with interfering ions, preventing them from reacting with the complexing agent. This allows the titration to selectively determine the metal ion of interest.
- Common masking reagents include cyanide ions (CN^-), which mask interfering metal ions such as copper, nickel, and zinc by forming stable complexes with them.

Demasking Reagents:

- Demasking reagents selectively release a metal ion from a complex, allowing it to react with the complexing agent.
- For example, EDTA can act as a demasking agent for calcium ions by forming a more stable complex with magnesium ions, thereby releasing calcium ions for titration.

Applications:

- Masking and demasking reagents are used in the analysis of complex samples containing multiple metal ions.
- They are particularly useful in environmental analysis, where samples may contain a variety of metal ions from natural and anthropogenic sources.

Considerations:

- The choice of masking or demasking reagent depends on the specific metal ions present in the sample and their interference with the titration.
- Care must be taken to ensure that the masking or demasking reaction does not interfere with the complexometric titration.

6.4 Estimation of Magnesium Sulphate and Calcium Gluconate

Magnesium sulfate and calcium gluconate are important pharmaceutical compounds used for various therapeutic purposes. The accurate estimation of these compounds is crucial to ensure the quality and efficacy of pharmaceutical formulations. Complexometric titrations are commonly employed for the estimation of magnesium and calcium ions in these compounds.

Estimation of Magnesium Sulphate:

- Magnesium sulfate is often present in pharmaceutical formulations as an electrolyte supplement or a laxative. It can be estimated by complexometric titration using EDTA as the complexing agent.
- In this titration, magnesium ions form a complex with EDTA, and the endpoint is detected using a metal ion indicator such as Eriochrome Black T.
- The reaction involved in the titration is: $Mg^{2+} + EDTA4^- \rightarrow Mg(EDTA)2$
- **Estimation of Calcium Gluconate:**

- Calcium gluconate is used as a calcium supplement in pharmaceutical formulations. It can also be estimated by complexometric titration using EDTA.
- The calcium ions in calcium gluconate form a complex with EDTA, and the endpoint is detected using a metal ion indicator.
- The reaction involved in the titration is: $Ca^{2+} + EDTA^{4-} \rightarrow Ca(EDTA)^{2-}$

Procedure:

1. Dissolve a known amount of the sample containing magnesium sulfate or calcium gluconate in water.
2. Add a suitable buffer solution to maintain the pH.
3. Titrate the solution with a standard solution of EDTA until the color changes, indicating the endpoint.
4. Note the volume of EDTA solution required for titration.
5. Calculate the concentration of magnesium sulfate or calcium gluconate based on the volume of EDTA used and the stoichiometry of the reaction.

Applications:

- The estimation of magnesium sulfate and calcium gluconate is essential in pharmaceutical quality control to ensure the proper formulation of medications.
- These estimations are also important in research and development to study the stability and compatibility of pharmaceutical formulations containing these compounds.

6.4.1 *Procedure and Calculations for Estimation of Magnesium Sulphate and Calcium Gluconate*

Estimation of Magnesium Sulphate:

1. **Procedure:**

   - Weigh accurately about 0.5 g of magnesium sulfate sample into a 250 mL conical flask.
   - Add about 50 mL of distilled water and 10 mL of ammonia buffer solution (pH 10).
   - Add a few drops of Eriochrome Black T indicator solution.
   - Titrate with standard EDTA solution until the color changes from wine-red to blue.
   - Note the volume of EDTA solution used.

2. **Calculations:**

   - The reaction involved in the titration is: $Mg^{2+} + EDTA^{4-} \rightarrow Mg(EDTA)2^{-}$
   - Calculate the moles of magnesium sulfate in the sample from the volume of EDTA used.
   - Calculate the concentration of magnesium sulfate in the sample solution.

Estimation of Calcium Gluconate:

1. **Procedure:**

- ○ Weigh accurately about 0.5 g of calcium gluconate sample into a 250 mL conical flask.
- ○ Add about 50 mL of distilled water and 10 mL of ammonia buffer solution (pH 10).
- ○ Add a few drops of Eriochrome Black T indicator solution.
- ○ Titrate with standard EDTA solution until the color changes from wine-red to blue.
- ○ Note the volume of EDTA solution used.

2. **Calculations:**

- ○ The reaction involved in the titration is: $Ca^{2+} + EDTA^{4-} \rightarrow Ca(EDTA)2^{-}$
- ○ Calculate the moles of calcium gluconate in the sample from the volume of EDTA used.
- ○ Calculate the concentration of calcium gluconate in the sample solution.

Applications:

- These procedures are used in pharmaceutical laboratories for the quality control of magnesium sulfate and calcium gluconate in drug formulations.
- The calculations are crucial for determining the exact concentration of these compounds in pharmaceutical products.

6.5 Gravimetric Analysis

Gravimetric analysis is a quantitative analytical method used to determine the concentration of an analyte in a sample based on the mass of a solid precipitate formed from the reaction between the analyte and a suitable reagent. This technique relies on the principle of stoichiometry and the law of conservation of mass.

Procedure:

1. **Sample Preparation:** The sample is dissolved in a suitable solvent, and any interfering substances are removed through appropriate treatments such as filtration or precipitation.

2. **Precipitation:** A reagent is added to the sample solution, causing the analyte to react and form a solid precipitate. The precipitate should be insoluble and easily filterable.
3. **Filtration:** The precipitate is separated from the solution by filtration using a filter paper or other suitable medium.
4. **Washing:** The precipitate is washed with a solvent to remove any impurities or soluble components.
5. **Drying:** The washed precipitate is dried to remove any residual moisture.
6. **Weighing:** The dried precipitate is weighed accurately using a sensitive balance.

Calculations:

- The mass of the precipitate is used to calculate the amount of analyte in the original sample based on the stoichiometry of the reaction.
- The concentration of the analyte is determined by dividing the mass of the precipitate by the volume of the sample and converting to the desired units.

Applications:

- Gravimetric analysis is widely used in environmental, pharmaceutical, and industrial laboratories for the determination of various analytes, including metal ions, organic compounds, and impurities.

Advantages:

- High precision and accuracy: Gravimetric analysis is a highly precise method that can achieve low detection limits and high levels of accuracy.
- Versatility: It can be applied to a wide range of analytes and sample matrices.
- Reliability: Gravimetric methods are based on fundamental principles of chemistry and are less susceptible to interference from other substances.

Challenges:

- Time-consuming: Gravimetric analysis often requires multiple steps and lengthy procedures, which can be time-consuming.

- Sensitivity to experimental conditions: Factors such as temperature, pH, and reaction time can affect the outcome of gravimetric analyses and must be carefully controlled.

6.5.1 *Principles and Steps Involved in Gravimetric Analysis*

Principles: Gravimetric analysis is based on the principle of quantitative precipitation of the analyte as a solid compound with a known stoichiometry. The mass of the precipitate is then used to calculate the amount of the analyte in the sample.

Steps Involved:

1. **Sample Preparation:** The sample is dissolved in a suitable solvent, and any insoluble impurities are removed by filtration.
2. **Precipitation:** A precipitating reagent is added to the sample solution, causing the analyte to form a solid compound. The choice of reagent depends on the analyte being determined.
3. **Digestion:** The mixture is heated or allowed to stand for a specific period to ensure the complete precipitation of the analyte.
4. **Filtration:** The precipitate is separated from the solution by filtration using a suitable filter paper.
5. **Washing:** The precipitate is washed with a suitable solvent to remove any soluble impurities.
6. **Drying:** The washed precipitate is dried to remove any remaining moisture.
7. **Ignition (if required):** Some precipitates require ignition to convert them to a stable form for weighing.
8. **Weighing:** The dried precipitate (or the ignited residue) is weighed using a sensitive analytical balance.
9. **Calculations:** The mass of the precipitate is used to calculate the amount of the analyte in the original sample using the stoichiometry of the reaction.

Applications:

- Gravimetric analysis is used for the determination of various analytes, including metal ions, organic compounds, and inorganic salts.
- It is widely used in environmental analysis, pharmaceutical analysis, and quality control in industries.

Advantages:

- High precision and accuracy: Gravimetric methods can achieve high levels of precision and accuracy.
- Universality: Gravimetric methods can be applied to a wide range of analytes.
- Reliability: Gravimetric methods are based on fundamental principles and are less susceptible to interference.

Challenges:

- Time-consuming: Gravimetric methods often require several hours to complete.
- Solubility issues: Some analytes may not precipitate quantitatively or may form soluble complexes.

6.5.3 Estimation of Barium Sulphate

Principle:

- Barium sulphate (BaSO4) is a highly insoluble compound that can be precipitated quantitatively from a solution containing barium ions.
- The precipitation reaction is: Ba^{2+} (aq)+SO_{42}–(aq)$\rightarrow$$BaSO_4(s)$
Procedure:

1. **Sample Preparation:** Dissolve the sample containing barium ions in water or acid.
2. **Precipitation:** Add an excess of a suitable sulphate solution (e.g., sulphuric acid or sodium sulphate) to the sample solution to ensure complete precipitation of barium ions as barium sulphate.
3. **Digestion:** Heat the mixture to ensure the complete precipitation of barium sulphate.

4. **Filtration:** Filter the precipitate through a weighed filter paper.
5. **Washing:** Wash the precipitate with distilled water to remove any soluble impurities.
6. **Drying:** Dry the precipitate at a suitable temperature to remove moisture.
7. **Weighing:** Weigh the dried precipitate on the filter paper using a sensitive balance.
8. **Calculations:** Calculate the mass of barium sulphate from the mass of the filter paper and the precipitate. From the mass of barium sulphate, calculate the amount of barium in the sample.

Applications:

- The estimation of barium sulphate is commonly used in environmental analysis, especially in the determination of barium in water samples.
- It is also used in the pharmaceutical industry for the quality control of barium-containing medications.

Redox Titrations
Principles:

- Redox titrations are based on the transfer of electrons between the analyte and the titrant.
- The endpoint of a redox titration is determined by a change in the oxidation state of the analyte, which is often indicated by a color change or by using a redox indicator.

Types of Redox Titrations:

1. **Cerimetry:** Involves the titration of a reducing agent with a standard solution of cerium(IV) sulphate.
2. **Iodimetry:** Involves the titration of an oxidizing agent with a standard solution of iodine.
3. **Iodometry:** Involves the titration of a reducing agent with a standard solution of iodine.
4. **Bromatometry:** Involves the titration of a reducing agent with a standard solution of bromine.

5. **Dichrometry:** Involves the titration of a reducing agent with a standard solution of potassium dichromate.
6. **Titration with Potassium Iodate:** Involves the titration of a reducing agent with a standard solution of potassium iodate.

Procedure:

- The procedure for a redox titration involves adding a titrant of known concentration to the analyte solution until the equivalence point is reached.
- The endpoint is often determined by using a suitable indicator or by monitoring a change in the physical properties of the solution, such as color change or change in potential.

Applications:

- Redox titrations are commonly used in the pharmaceutical industry for the analysis of drugs and pharmaceutical products.
- They are also used in environmental analysis for the determination of pollutants in water and air samples.

Advantages:

- Redox titrations are versatile and can be applied to a wide range of analytes.
- They are relatively simple and quick to perform compared to other analytical techniques.

Challenges:

- Redox titrations can be affected by side reactions, which can lead to errors in the results.
- The choice of indicator is critical and can affect the accuracy of the titration.

Conclusion: Redox titrations are an important analytical technique used in various industries for the quantitative analysis of a wide range of analytes. Despite their challenges, they offer high precision and accuracy, making them valuable tools in analytical chemistry.

CHAPTER VII

Redox Titrations

7.1 Concepts of Oxidation and Reduction

Definitions and Principles:

- **Oxidation:** Oxidation is the loss of electrons by a substance, leading to an increase in its oxidation state. In the context of redox reactions, oxidation involves the transfer of electrons from one substance to another.
- **Reduction:** Reduction is the gain of electrons by a substance, leading to a decrease in its oxidation state. Redox reactions always involve both oxidation and reduction processes.

Oxidation State: The oxidation state of an element in a compound indicates the number of electrons that an atom has gained or lost relative to its neutral state. It is a measure of the degree of oxidation of an atom in a compound.

Rules for Assigning Oxidation States:

1. The oxidation state of an atom in its elemental form is zero.
2. The oxidation state of a monatomic ion is equal to its charge.
3. In compounds, the sum of oxidation states of all atoms is equal to the overall charge of the compound.
4. In most compounds, oxygen has an oxidation state of -2, and hydrogen has an oxidation state of +1.
5. Fluorine always has an oxidation state of -1 in compounds.

Redox Reactions:

- Redox reactions are chemical reactions that involve the transfer of electrons between reactants.
- The substance that undergoes oxidation is called the reducing agent, as it causes the reduction of another substance.

- The substance that undergoes reduction is called the oxidizing agent, as it causes the oxidation of another substance.

Importance in Analytical Chemistry:

- Understanding oxidation and reduction is crucial in redox titrations, where the endpoint of the titration is determined by the redox reaction between the analyte and the titrant.
- In pharmaceutical analysis, redox reactions are used for the determination of drugs and impurities in pharmaceutical formulations.

7.1.2 Oxidation-Reduction Reactions

Definition: Oxidation-reduction (redox) reactions are chemical reactions in which electrons are transferred between reactants, leading to changes in the oxidation states of the elements involved.

Key Concepts:

- **Oxidation:** In redox reactions, oxidation refers to the loss of electrons by a substance. This results in an increase in the oxidation state of the element undergoing oxidation.
- **Reduction:** Reduction involves the gain of electrons by a substance, leading to a decrease in its oxidation state.

Examples:

1. **Combustion Reactions:** Combustion reactions are a common example of redox reactions where a substance reacts with oxygen, resulting in the release of energy. For example, the combustion of methane (CH_4) can be represented as: $CH_4(g)+2O_2(g) \rightarrow CO_2(g)+2H_2O(l)$
2. In this reaction, methane is oxidized to carbon dioxide, and oxygen is reduced to water.
3. **Corrosion:** The rusting of iron is another example of a redox reaction. Iron reacts with oxygen and water to form iron oxide (rust). The reaction can be represented as: $4Fe(s)+3O_2(g)+6H_2O(l) \rightarrow 4Fe(OH)_3(s)$
4. **Electrochemical Cells:** Redox reactions are also central to the functioning of electrochemical cells, such as batteries and fuel cells,

where chemical energy is converted into electrical energy through redox reactions.

Applications:

- Redox reactions play a crucial role in various industrial processes, such as the production of metals, bleaching of materials, and in the pharmaceutical industry for synthesis and analysis.
- Understanding redox reactions is important in environmental chemistry for studying processes like oxidation of pollutants and detoxification of contaminants.

Conclusion: Oxidation-reduction reactions are fundamental in chemistry and have wide-ranging applications. They are key to understanding energy transfer in chemical reactions and are central to many important processes in nature and industry.

7.2 Types of Redox Titrations

Introduction: Redox titrations are a class of analytical techniques used to determine the concentration of an analyte by measuring the volume of a titrant required to complete a redox reaction. These titrations are based on the transfer of electrons between the reactants, leading to changes in oxidation states. Various types of redox titrations are employed in analytical chemistry, each with its own set of principles and applications.

Types of Redox Titrations:

1. **Cerimetric Titrations:**

   ◦ **Principle:** In cerimetric titrations, cerium(IV) sulfate $(Ce(SO4)_2$ is used as the titrant. Cerium(IV) is reduced to cerium(III) by the analyte.

   ◦ **Applications:** Cerimetric titrations are commonly used for the determination of reducing agents in pharmaceuticals, food products, and environmental samples.

$$Ce^{4+} + e^{-} \rightarrow Ce^{3+}$$

Iodimetric Titrations:

- ○ **Principle:** Iodimetric titrations involve the use of iodine as the titrant. Iodine is reduced to iodide ion by the analyte.
- ○ **Applications:** Iodimetric titrations are used for the determination of oxidizing agents, such as chlorine, bromine, and certain pharmaceuticals.

$I_2 + 2e^- \rightarrow 2I^-$

Iodometric Titrations:

- ○ **Principle:** In iodometric titrations, iodide ion is oxidized to iodine by the analyte.
- ○ **Applications:** Iodometric titrations are used for the determination of reducing agents, such as thiosulfate, sulfites, and certain pharmaceuticals.

$2I^- \rightarrow I_2 + 2e^-$

Bromatometric Titrations:

- ○ **Principle:** Bromatometric titrations involve the use of bromine as the titrant. Bromine is reduced to bromide ion by the analyte.
- ○ **Applications:** Bromatometric titrations are used for the determination of reducing agents, such as thiosulfate, sulfites, and certain pharmaceuticals.

$Br_2 + 2e^- \rightarrow 2Br^-$

Dichrometric Titrations:

- ○ **Principle:** Dichrometric titrations involve the use of potassium dichromate as the titrant. Dichromate ion is reduced to chromium(III) ion by the analyte.
- ○ **Applications:** Dichrometric titrations are used for the determination of reducing agents, such as ferrous ion, hydrogen peroxide, and certain pharmaceuticals.

$Cr_2O_7^{2-} + 6e^- + 14H^+ \rightarrow 2Cr3^+ + 7H_2O$

1. **Titration with Potassium Iodate:**

- **Principle:** This titration involves the use of potassium iodate as the titrant. Iodate ion is reduced to iodine by the analyte.
- **Applications:** Titration with potassium iodate is used for the determination of reducing agents, such as ascorbic acid and certain pharmaceuticals.

$$IO_3^- + 5I^- + 6H^+ \rightarrow 3I_2 + 3H_2O$$

7.2.1 Cerimetry

Introduction: Cerimetry is a type of redox titration that involves the use of cerium(IV) sulfate $(Ce(SO_4)_2$ as the titrant. Cerium(IV) is a powerful oxidizing agent and is reduced to cerium(III) during the titration process. Cerimetry is widely used for the determination of reducing agents in various industries, including pharmaceuticals, environmental analysis, and food industry.

Principle: In cerimetry, the analyte (reducing agent) reacts with cerium(IV) ions in acidic medium, leading to the reduction of cerium(IV) to cerium(III). The reaction is typically monitored using a suitable indicator that changes color at the endpoint of the titration.

Applications: Cerimetry finds applications in the determination of various reducing agents, including:

- Ascorbic acid in pharmaceutical formulations
- Sulfur dioxide in wine and food products
- Hydrogen peroxide in bleach solutions
- Iron(II) ions in environmental samples

Procedure:

1. Preparation of the cerium(IV) solution: Cerium(IV) sulfate is prepared by dissolving cerium(IV) oxide in dilute sulfuric acid.
2. Titration: The analyte solution is added to the cerium(IV) solution, and the reaction is allowed to proceed to the endpoint.
3. Endpoint detection: The endpoint of the titration is typically detected using a visual indicator that changes color when all the cerium(IV) ions are reduced to cerium(III).

Example Reaction: The reaction between cerium(IV) and a reducing agent (e.g., ascorbic acid) can be represented as follows: Ce^{4+}Ascorbic acid$\rightarrow Ce^{3+}$ +Dehydroascorbic acid

7.2.2 Iodimetry and Iodometry

Introduction: Iodimetry and iodometry are two related titration techniques based on the redox reaction involving iodine and an oxidizing or reducing agent, respectively. These methods are widely used in analytical chemistry for the quantitative determination of substances that can oxidize or reduce iodine.

Iodimetry:

- **Principle:** Iodimetry involves the titration of an oxidizing agent with a solution of iodide ions (I^-) to liberate iodine, which is then titrated with a standard solution of a reducing agent.
- **Applications:** Iodimetry is used for the determination of oxidizing agents such as chlorine, bromine, and certain pharmaceuticals.

Example Reaction (Iodimetry): $2Cl^-+Cl_2\rightarrow 3I^-+2Cl^-$
Iodometry:

- **Principle:** Iodometry, on the other hand, involves the titration of a reducing agent with a solution of iodine in the presence of a starch indicator.
- **Applications:** Iodometry is used for the determination of reducing agents such as thiosulfate, sulfites, and certain pharmaceuticals.

Example Reaction (Iodometry): $2S_2O3^{2-}+I_2\rightarrow S_4O6^{2-}+2I^-$
Procedure:

1. **Preparation of Solutions:** Prepare standard solutions of iodine and iodide ions.
2. **Titration:** Add the iodine solution to the analyte solution until a faint color persists.
3. **Endpoint Detection:** Add starch indicator, which forms a blue complex with iodine. The appearance of a blue color indicates the endpoint.

7.2.3 Bromatometry

Introduction: Bromatometry is a redox titration method that involves the use of bromine as the titrant. Similar to iodimetry and iodometry, bromatometry is used for the quantitative determination of substances that can oxidize or reduce bromine.

Principle: In bromatometry, the analyte is titrated with a solution of bromine, which is reduced to bromide ions in the presence of excess bromide ions and an acid. The reaction is monitored using a suitable indicator, such as starch, which forms a blue complex with bromine.

Applications: Bromatometry is commonly used for the determination of reducing agents, such as thiosulfate, sulfites, and certain pharmaceuticals, similar to iodometry.

Example Reaction: $2S_2O_3^{2-} + Br^2 \rightarrow S_4O_62^- + 2Br^-$

Procedure:

1. **Preparation of Solutions:** Prepare standard solutions of bromine and bromide ions.
2. **Titration:** Add the bromine solution to the analyte solution until a faint color persists.
3. **Endpoint Detection:** Add starch indicator, which forms a blue complex with bromine. The appearance of a blue color indicates the endpoint.

7.2.4 Dichrometry

Introduction: Dichrometry is a redox titration technique that utilizes potassium dichromate ($K_2Cr_2O_7$) as the titrant. This method is commonly used for the quantitative determination of substances that can be oxidized by dichromate ions under acidic conditions.

Principle: In dichrometry, the analyte is titrated with a solution of potassium dichromate in the presence of an indicator that changes color at the endpoint. The reaction involves the reduction of dichromate ions to chromium(III) ions.

Applications: Dichrometry is used for the determination of various substances, including ferrous ions, hydrogen peroxide, and certain pharmaceuticals, which can be oxidized by dichromate ions.

Example Reaction: $Cr_2O7^{2-}+6Fe2^++14H^+\rightarrow 2Cr^{3+}+6Fe3^++7H_2O$
Procedure:

1. **Preparation of Solutions:** Prepare standard solutions of potassium dichromate and the analyte.
2. **Titration:** Add the potassium dichromate solution to the analyte solution until the endpoint is reached.
3. **Endpoint Detection:** Use a suitable indicator to detect the endpoint, which is typically a color change.

7.2.5 Titration with Potassium Iodate

Introduction: Titration with potassium iodate is a redox titration method used for the quantitative determination of reducing agents. In this method, potassium iodate (KIO_3) is used as the titrant, and the reaction involves the reduction of iodate ions ($IO3^-$) to iodine (I_2).

Principle: The analyte is titrated with a solution of potassium iodate in the presence of an indicator that changes color at the endpoint. The reduction of iodate ions to iodine is typically carried out in an acidic medium.

Applications: Titration with potassium iodate is used for the determination of various reducing agents, including arsenic, sulfites, and certain pharmaceuticals.

Example Reaction: $IO^{3-}+5I^-+6H^+\rightarrow 3I_2+3H_2O$
Procedure:

1. **Preparation of Solutions:** Prepare standard solutions of potassium iodate and the analyte.
2. **Titration:** Add the potassium iodate solution to the analyte solution until the endpoint is reached.
3. **Endpoint Detection:** Use a suitable indicator to detect the endpoint, which is typically a color change from colorless to pale yellow (due to the formation of iodine).

7.3 Applications in Pharmaceutical Analysis

7.3.1 Examples and Case Studies

Introduction: Pharmaceutical analysis plays a crucial role in ensuring the quality, safety, and efficacy of pharmaceutical products. Redox titration techniques, such as iodimetry, iodometry, bromatometry, dichrometry, and titration with potassium iodate, find wide applications in pharmaceutical analysis for the determination of various substances. Here, we discuss some examples and case studies highlighting the application of these techniques in pharmaceutical analysis.

Example 1: Determination of Ascorbic Acid (Vitamin C) Content in Pharmaceutical Formulations

- **Technique:** Iodometric Titration
- **Procedure:** Ascorbic acid is titrated with iodine in the presence of starch indicator. The endpoint is indicated by the disappearance of the blue starch-iodine complex.
- **Application:** This method is used to determine the ascorbic acid content in vitamin C tablets and syrups.

Example 2: Quantification of Thiosulfate in Pharmaceutical Solutions

- **Technique:** Iodimetry
- **Procedure:** Thiosulfate is titrated with iodine in acidic medium. The endpoint is detected by the appearance of a faint yellow color due to the formation of iodine-starch complex.
- **Application:** This method is used to determine the thiosulfate content in pharmaceutical solutions, such as eye drops.

Example 3: Estimation of Sulfites in Pharmaceutical Preparations

- **Technique:** Iodometric Titration
- **Procedure:** Sulfites are titrated with iodine in the presence of starch indicator. The endpoint is indicated by the disappearance of the blue starch-iodine complex.
- **Application:** This method is used to quantify sulfites in pharmaceutical formulations, such as liquid medicines.

Case Study: Determination of Iron Content in Iron Supplements

- **Technique:** Dichrometry
- **Procedure:** Iron in the supplement is oxidized to ferric ions by potassium dichromate in acidic medium. The unreacted dichromate is back-titrated with a standard solution of ferrous ammonium sulfate.
- **Application:** This method is used to determine the iron content in iron supplements, ensuring that the product meets the required specifications.

Conclusion: These examples and case studies demonstrate the versatility and importance of redox titration techniques in pharmaceutical analysis. By employing these methods, pharmaceutical analysts can accurately determine the concentration of various substances in pharmaceutical formulations, ensuring their quality and efficacy.

7.1 Concepts of Oxidation and Reduction

Definitions and Principles:

- **Oxidation:** Oxidation is the loss of electrons by a substance, leading to an increase in its oxidation state. In the context of redox reactions, oxidation involves the transfer of electrons from one substance to another.
- **Reduction:** Reduction is the gain of electrons by a substance, leading to a decrease in its oxidation state. Redox reactions always involve both oxidation and reduction processes.

Oxidation State: The oxidation state of an element in a compound indicates the number of electrons that an atom has gained or lost relative to its neutral state. It is a measure of the degree of oxidation of an atom in a compound.

Rules for Assigning Oxidation States:

1. The oxidation state of an atom in its elemental form is zero.
2. The oxidation state of a monatomic ion is equal to its charge.
3. In compounds, the sum of oxidation states of all atoms is equal to the overall charge of the compound.
4. In most compounds, oxygen has an oxidation state of -2, and hydrogen has an oxidation state of +1.
5. Fluorine always has an oxidation state of -1 in compounds.

Redox Reactions:

- Redox reactions are chemical reactions that involve the transfer of electrons between reactants.
- The substance that undergoes oxidation is called the reducing agent, as it causes the reduction of another substance.
- The substance that undergoes reduction is called the oxidizing agent, as it causes the oxidation of another substance.

Importance in Analytical Chemistry:

- Understanding oxidation and reduction is crucial in redox titrations, where the endpoint of the titration is determined by the redox reaction between the analyte and the titrant.
- In pharmaceutical analysis, redox reactions are used for the determination of drugs and impurities in pharmaceutical formulations.

7.1.2 Oxidation-Reduction Reactions

Definition: Oxidation-reduction (redox) reactions are chemical reactions in which electrons are transferred between reactants, leading to changes in the oxidation states of the elements involved.

Key Concepts:

- **Oxidation:** In redox reactions, oxidation refers to the loss of electrons by a substance. This results in an increase in the oxidation state of the element undergoing oxidation.
- **Reduction:** Reduction involves the gain of electrons by a substance, leading to a decrease in its oxidation state.

Examples:

1. **Combustion Reactions:** Combustion reactions are a common example of redox reactions where a substance reacts with oxygen, resulting in the release of energy. For example, the combustion of methane (CH_4) can be represented as: $CH_4(g) + 2O_2(g) \rightarrow CO_2(g) + 2H_2O(l)$
2. In this reaction, methane is oxidized to carbon dioxide, and oxygen is reduced to water.

3. **Corrosion:** The rusting of iron is another example of a redox reaction. Iron reacts with oxygen and water to form iron oxide (rust). The reaction can be represented as: $4Fe(s)+3O_2(g)+6H_2O(l)\rightarrow4Fe(OH)_3(s)$
4. **Electrochemical Cells:** Redox reactions are also central to the functioning of electrochemical cells, such as batteries and fuel cells, where chemical energy is converted into electrical energy through redox reactions.

Applications:

- Redox reactions play a crucial role in various industrial processes, such as the production of metals, bleaching of materials, and in the pharmaceutical industry for synthesis and analysis.
- Understanding redox reactions is important in environmental chemistry for studying processes like oxidation of pollutants and detoxification of contaminants.

Conclusion: Oxidation-reduction reactions are fundamental in chemistry and have wide-ranging applications. They are key to understanding energy transfer in chemical reactions and are central to many important processes in nature and industry.

7.2 Types of Redox Titrations

Introduction: Redox titrations are a class of analytical techniques used to determine the concentration of an analyte by measuring the volume of a titrant required to complete a redox reaction. These titrations are based on the transfer of electrons between the reactants, leading to changes in oxidation states. Various types of redox titrations are employed in analytical chemistry, each with its own set of principles and applications.

Types of Redox Titrations:

1. **Cerimetric Titrations:**

   - **Principle:** In cerimetric titrations, cerium(IV) sulfate ($Ce(SO4)_2$ is used as the titrant. Cerium(IV) is reduced to cerium(III) by the analyte.
   - **Applications:** Cerimetric titrations are commonly used for the determination of reducing agents in pharmaceuticals, food products, and environmental samples.

$Ce4^+ + e- \rightarrow Ce^{3+}$

Iodimetric Titrations:

- **Principle:** Iodimetric titrations involve the use of iodine as the titrant. Iodine is reduced to iodide ion by the analyte.
- **Applications:** Iodimetric titrations are used for the determination of oxidizing agents, such as chlorine, bromine, and certain pharmaceuticals.

$I_2 + 2e^- \rightarrow 2I^-$

Iodometric Titrations:

- **Principle:** In iodometric titrations, iodide ion is oxidized to iodine by the analyte.
- **Applications:** Iodometric titrations are used for the determination of reducing agents, such as thiosulfate, sulfites, and certain pharmaceuticals.

$2I- \rightarrow I_2 + 2e^-$

Bromatometric Titrations:

- **Principle:** Bromatometric titrations involve the use of bromine as the titrant. Bromine is reduced to bromide ion by the analyte.
- **Applications:** Bromatometric titrations are used for the determination of reducing agents, such as thiosulfate, sulfites, and certain pharmaceuticals.

$Br_2 + 2e^- \rightarrow 2Br^-$

Dichrometric Titrations:

- **Principle:** Dichrometric titrations involve the use of potassium dichromate as the titrant. Dichromate ion is reduced to chromium(III) ion by the analyte.
- **Applications:** Dichrometric titrations are used for the determination of reducing agents, such as ferrous ion, hydrogen peroxide, and certain pharmaceuticals.

$Cr_2O_7^{2-}+6e^-+14H^+\rightarrow2Cr3^++7H_2O$

1. **Titration with Potassium Iodate:**

   - **Principle:** This titration involves the use of potassium iodate as the titrant. Iodate ion is reduced to iodine by the analyte.
   - **Applications:** Titration with potassium iodate is used for the determination of reducing agents, such as ascorbic acid and certain pharmaceuticals.

$IO_3^-+5I^-+6H^+\rightarrow3I_2+3H_2O$

7.2.1 Cerimetry

Introduction: Cerimetry is a type of redox titration that involves the use of cerium(IV) sulfate ($Ce(SO_4)_2$ as the titrant. Cerium(IV) is a powerful oxidizing agent and is reduced to cerium(III) during the titration process. Cerimetry is widely used for the determination of reducing agents in various industries, including pharmaceuticals, environmental analysis, and food industry.

Principle: In cerimetry, the analyte (reducing agent) reacts with cerium(IV) ions in acidic medium, leading to the reduction of cerium(IV) to cerium(III). The reaction is typically monitored using a suitable indicator that changes color at the endpoint of the titration.

Applications: Cerimetry finds applications in the determination of various reducing agents, including:

- Ascorbic acid in pharmaceutical formulations
- Sulfur dioxide in wine and food products
- Hydrogen peroxide in bleach solutions
- Iron(II) ions in environmental samples

Procedure:

1. Preparation of the cerium(IV) solution: Cerium(IV) sulfate is prepared by dissolving cerium(IV) oxide in dilute sulfuric acid.
2. Titration: The analyte solution is added to the cerium(IV) solution, and the reaction is allowed to proceed to the endpoint.
3. Endpoint detection: The endpoint of the titration is typically detected using a visual indicator that changes color when all the cerium(IV) ions

are reduced to cerium(III).

Example Reaction: The reaction between cerium(IV) and a reducing agent (e.g., ascorbic acid) can be represented as follows: Ce^{4+}+Ascorbic acid$\rightarrow Ce^{3+}$ +Dehydroascorbic acid

7.2.2 Iodimetry and Iodometry

Introduction: Iodimetry and iodometry are two related titration techniques based on the redox reaction involving iodine and an oxidizing or reducing agent, respectively. These methods are widely used in analytical chemistry for the quantitative determination of substances that can oxidize or reduce iodine.

Iodimetry:

- **Principle:** Iodimetry involves the titration of an oxidizing agent with a solution of iodide ions (I^-) to liberate iodine, which is then titrated with a standard solution of a reducing agent.
- **Applications:** Iodimetry is used for the determination of oxidizing agents such as chlorine, bromine, and certain pharmaceuticals.

Example Reaction (Iodimetry): $2Cl^-+Cl_2\rightarrow 3I^-+2Cl^-$

Iodometry:

- **Principle:** Iodometry, on the other hand, involves the titration of a reducing agent with a solution of iodine in the presence of a starch indicator.
- **Applications:** Iodometry is used for the determination of reducing agents such as thiosulfate, sulfites, and certain pharmaceuticals.

Example Reaction (Iodometry): $2S_2O3^{2-}+I_2\rightarrow S_4O6^{2-}+2I^-$

Procedure:

1. **Preparation of Solutions:** Prepare standard solutions of iodine and iodide ions.
2. **Titration:** Add the iodine solution to the analyte solution until a faint color persists.
3. **Endpoint Detection:** Add starch indicator, which forms a blue complex with iodine. The appearance of a blue color indicates the endpoint.

7.2.3 Bromatometry

Introduction: Bromatometry is a redox titration method that involves the use of bromine as the titrant. Similar to iodimetry and iodometry, bromatometry is used for the quantitative determination of substances that can oxidize or reduce bromine.

Principle: In bromatometry, the analyte is titrated with a solution of bromine, which is reduced to bromide ions in the presence of excess bromide ions and an acid. The reaction is monitored using a suitable indicator, such as starch, which forms a blue complex with bromine.

Applications: Bromatometry is commonly used for the determination of reducing agents, such as thiosulfate, sulfites, and certain pharmaceuticals, similar to iodometry.

Example Reaction: $2S_2O_3^{2-} + Br_2 \rightarrow S_4O_6^{2-} + 2Br^-$

Procedure:

1. **Preparation of Solutions:** Prepare standard solutions of bromine and bromide ions.
2. **Titration:** Add the bromine solution to the analyte solution until a faint color persists.
3. **Endpoint Detection:** Add starch indicator, which forms a blue complex with bromine. The appearance of a blue color indicates the endpoint.

7.2.4 Dichrometry

Introduction: Dichrometry is a redox titration technique that utilizes potassium dichromate ($K_2Cr_2O_7$) as the titrant. This method is commonly used for the quantitative determination of substances that can be oxidized by dichromate ions under acidic conditions.

Principle: In dichrometry, the analyte is titrated with a solution of potassium dichromate in the presence of an indicator that changes color at the endpoint. The reaction involves the reduction of dichromate ions to chromium(III) ions.

Applications: Dichrometry is used for the determination of various substances, including ferrous ions, hydrogen peroxide, and certain pharmaceuticals, which can be oxidized by dichromate ions.

Example Reaction: $Cr_2O_7^{2-} + 6Fe^{2+} + 14H^+ \rightarrow 2Cr^{3+} + 6Fe^{3+} + 7H_2O$

Procedure:

1. **Preparation of Solutions:** Prepare standard solutions of potassium dichromate and the analyte.
2. **Titration:** Add the potassium dichromate solution to the analyte solution until the endpoint is reached.
3. **Endpoint Detection:** Use a suitable indicator to detect the endpoint, which is typically a color change.

7.2.5 Titration with Potassium Iodate

Introduction: Titration with potassium iodate is a redox titration method used for the quantitative determination of reducing agents. In this method, potassium iodate (KIO_3) is used as the titrant, and the reaction involves the reduction of iodate ions ($IO3^-$) to iodine (I_2).

Principle: The analyte is titrated with a solution of potassium iodate in the presence of an indicator that changes color at the endpoint. The reduction of iodate ions to iodine is typically carried out in an acidic medium.

Applications: Titration with potassium iodate is used for the determination of various reducing agents, including arsenic, sulfites, and certain pharmaceuticals.

Example Reaction: $IO^{3-}+5I^-+6H^+ \rightarrow 3I_2+3H_2O$

Procedure:

1. **Preparation of Solutions:** Prepare standard solutions of potassium iodate and the analyte.
2. **Titration:** Add the potassium iodate solution to the analyte solution until the endpoint is reached.
3. **Endpoint Detection:** Use a suitable indicator to detect the endpoint, which is typically a color change from colorless to pale yellow (due to the formation of iodine).

7.3 Applications in Pharmaceutical Analysis
7.3.1 Examples and Case Studies

Introduction: Pharmaceutical analysis plays a crucial role in ensuring the quality, safety, and efficacy of pharmaceutical products. Redox titration techniques, such as iodimetry, iodometry, bromatometry, dichrometry, and titration with potassium iodate, find wide applications in pharmaceutical analysis for the determination of various substances. Here, we discuss some examples and case studies highlighting the application of these techniques in pharmaceutical analysis.

Example 1: Determination of Ascorbic Acid (Vitamin C) Content in Pharmaceutical Formulations

- **Technique:** Iodometric Titration
- **Procedure:** Ascorbic acid is titrated with iodine in the presence of starch indicator. The endpoint is indicated by the disappearance of the blue starch-iodine complex.
- **Application:** This method is used to determine the ascorbic acid content in vitamin C tablets and syrups.

Example 2: Quantification of Thiosulfate in Pharmaceutical Solutions

- **Technique:** Iodimetry
- **Procedure:** Thiosulfate is titrated with iodine in acidic medium. The endpoint is detected by the appearance of a faint yellow color due to the formation of iodine-starch complex.
- **Application:** This method is used to determine the thiosulfate content in pharmaceutical solutions, such as eye drops.

Example 3: Estimation of Sulfites in Pharmaceutical Preparations

- **Technique:** Iodometric Titration
- **Procedure:** Sulfites are titrated with iodine in the presence of starch indicator. The endpoint is indicated by the disappearance of the blue starch-iodine complex.
- **Application:** This method is used to quantify sulfites in pharmaceutical formulations, such as liquid medicines.

Case Study: Determination of Iron Content in Iron Supplements

- **Technique:** Dichrometry
- **Procedure:** Iron in the supplement is oxidized to ferric ions by potassium dichromate in acidic medium. The unreacted dichromate is back-titrated with a standard solution of ferrous ammonium sulfate.
- **Application:** This method is used to determine the iron content in iron supplements, ensuring that the product meets the required specifications.

These examples and case studies demonstrate the versatility and importance of redox titration techniques in pharmaceutical analysis. By employing these methods, pharmaceutical analysts can accurately determine the concentration of various substances in pharmaceutical formulations, ensuring their quality and efficacy.

CHAPTER VIII

Electrochemical Methods of Analysis

8.1 Conductometry

8.1.1 Introduction and Principles

Introduction: Conductometry is a widely used analytical technique in pharmaceutical analysis for determining the concentration of ions in a solution. It is based on the measurement of the electrical conductivity of a solution, which depends on the ability of ions to carry an electrical current.

Principles: The principle behind conductometry is Ohm's Law, which states that the electrical current (I) flowing through a conductor is directly proportional to the voltage (V) across the conductor, and inversely proportional to the resistance (R) of the conductor. In the case of a solution, the conductivity (κ) is related to the concentration of ions and their mobility in the solution.

The conductivity of a solution can be expressed as:

$$\kappa = \lambda \times F \times C \,/\, A$$

Where:

- κ is the conductivity of the solution
- λ is the molar conductivity of the ions in the solution
- F is the Faraday constant (96,485 C/mol)
- C is the concentration of the ions in the solution
- A is the area of the electrodes

During a titration, the conductivity of the solution changes as the titrant is added. At the endpoint of the titration, there is a sudden change in conductivity, indicating that the reaction is complete. This change in conductivity is used to determine the endpoint of the titration.

8.1.2 Conductivity Cells

Introduction: Conductivity cells are devices used to measure the electrical conductivity of a solution. They consist of two electrodes immersed in the solution, and the conductivity is measured based on the electrical resistance between these electrodes.

Types of Conductivity Cells:

1. **Conductivity Cell with Platinum Electrodes:** These cells use platinum electrodes that are inert and resistant to corrosion. They are suitable for a wide range of conductivity measurements.
2. **Conductivity Cell with Glass Electrodes:** Glass electrodes are used in cells designed for measurements in non-aqueous solutions or solutions containing organic solvents.
3. **Conductivity Cell with Metal Electrodes:** Metal electrodes, such as stainless steel or graphite, are used in cells for measurements in solutions that are not compatible with platinum electrodes.

Cell Constants: The cell constant (K) of a conductivity cell is a factor used to convert the measured conductivity to the actual conductivity of the solution. It is determined by the geometry of the cell and the distance between the electrodes.

Maintenance and Calibration: Conductivity cells require regular maintenance and calibration to ensure accurate measurements. This includes cleaning the electrodes, checking for any damage or corrosion, and calibrating the cell using standard solutions of known conductivity.

8.1.3 Conductometric Titrations

Introduction: Conductometric titration is a method used in analytical chemistry to determine the endpoint of a titration by measuring the conductivity of the solution. It is based on the principle that the conductivity of a solution changes as titrant is added to the analyte solution, and this change can be used to detect the endpoint of the titration.

Principle: During a conductometric titration, the conductivity of the solution changes due to the formation or consumption of ions. At the beginning of the titration, the conductivity is high because both the analyte and titrant are present in their ionic forms. As the titrant is added, it reacts with the analyte to form a less conductive product. The endpoint of the titration is reached when the conductivity undergoes a sudden change, indicating that the reaction is complete.

Applications: Conductometric titrations are commonly used in pharmaceutical analysis for the determination of various substances, including acids, bases, and salts. They are particularly useful for titrations involving weak acids or bases, where the pH change at the endpoint is not very pronounced.

Procedure:

1. Prepare the analyte solution in a suitable solvent.
2. Add a small amount of a suitable indicator to the analyte solution, if necessary.
3. Titrate the analyte solution with the titrant while monitoring the conductivity of the solution.
4. Note the volume of titrant added when the conductivity undergoes a sudden change, indicating the endpoint of the titration.

8.1.4 Applications in Pharmaceutical Analysis

Introduction: Conductometry finds wide applications in pharmaceutical analysis due to its sensitivity, simplicity, and ability to provide real-time monitoring of reactions. It is particularly useful in titrations and other analytical procedures where the concentration of ions needs to be determined.

Applications:

1. **Endpoint Detection in Acid-Base Titrations:** Conductometry is commonly used to detect the endpoint of acid-base titrations by monitoring the change in conductivity as the titrant is added. This method is particularly useful for titrations involving weak acids or bases where the pH change at the endpoint is not very pronounced.
2. **Determination of Conductivity of Solutions:** Conductometry is used to determine the conductivity of pharmaceutical solutions, which can provide information about the ionic strength and composition of the solution.
3. **Monitoring of Reaction Progress:** Conductometry can be used to monitor the progress of reactions in pharmaceutical formulations. For example, it can be used to monitor the formation of complexes in complexometric titrations or the precipitation of salts in precipitation

reactions.

4. **Quality Control of Pharmaceutical Formulations:** Conductometry is used in the quality control of pharmaceutical formulations to ensure that they meet the required specifications. For example, it can be used to determine the concentration of active ingredients or the presence of impurities in a formulation.

8.2 Potentiometry

Introduction: Potentiometry is an analytical technique used to measure the voltage (or potential) difference between two electrodes in a solution. It is widely used in pharmaceutical analysis for determining the concentration of ions, pH, and other properties of solutions.

Principle: Potentiometry is based on the principle that the potential difference between two electrodes in a solution is proportional to the concentration of ions in the solution. This potential difference is measured using a voltmeter and a reference electrode.

Applications:

1. **pH Measurement:** Potentiometry is commonly used to measure the pH of a solution. A glass electrode is used as the sensing electrode, and a reference electrode (such as a silver-silver chloride electrode) is used as the reference.

2. **Ion Selective Electrodes:** Potentiometry can be used with ion-selective electrodes to measure the concentration of specific ions in a solution. These electrodes are selective to specific ions and can provide selective measurements.

3. **Endpoint Detection in Titrations:** Potentiometry can be used to detect the endpoint of acid-base titrations by monitoring the change in potential as the titrant is added. This method is particularly useful for titrations where the pH change at the endpoint is not very pronounced.

4. **Determination of Drug Concentrations:** Potentiometry can be used to determine the concentration of drugs in pharmaceutical formulations. This is done by measuring the potential change when the drug reacts with a specific ion-selective electrode.

8.2.1 Electrochemical Cells

Introduction: Electrochemical cells are devices used in potentiometry to measure the voltage difference between two electrodes in a solution. They consist of two electrodes - a working electrode and a reference electrode - immersed in the solution of interest.

Types of Electrochemical Cells:

1. **Galvanic Cells:** These cells generate electrical energy from spontaneous chemical reactions. They consist of two half-cells connected by a salt bridge, with each half-cell containing an electrode immersed in an electrolyte solution.
2. **Electrolytic Cells:** These cells use electrical energy to drive non-spontaneous chemical reactions. They consist of two electrodes connected to an external power source, with the reaction occurring at the electrodes driven by the applied voltage.
3. **Concentration Cells:** These cells measure the difference in concentration of ions between two solutions. They consist of two half-cells with the same electrode material but different ion concentrations, leading to a potential difference between the two half-cells.

Components of an Electrochemical Cell:

- **Working Electrode:** The electrode where the reaction of interest occurs.
- **Reference Electrode:** The electrode with a stable and known electrode potential, used as a reference for the working electrode.
- **Electrolyte Solution:** The solution in which the electrodes are immersed, containing ions that participate in the electrochemical reaction.

Applications in Pharmaceutical Analysis:

- Electrochemical cells are used in potentiometry to measure pH, determine concentrations of ions, and detect endpoints in titrations.
- They are also used in the development and quality control of pharmaceutical formulations to ensure that they meet the required specifications.

8.2.2 Reference Electrodes

Introduction: Reference electrodes are a critical component in potentiometric measurements, providing a stable and known potential against which the potential of the working electrode is measured. They play a pivotal role in ensuring accurate and reproducible results in electrochemical analysis.

Types of Reference Electrodes:

1. **Standard Hydrogen Electrode (SHE):**

   - **Principle:** The SHE is based on the redox reaction involving hydrogen gas and hydrogen ions in an acidic solution. It is the primary reference electrode with an assigned potential of 0.00 volts at all temperatures.
   - **Construction:** It consists of a platinum electrode in contact with 1 M HCl solution, through which hydrogen gas is bubbled.
   - **Applications:** Although highly accurate, it is rarely used in routine analysis due to its cumbersome setup and maintenance.

2. **Silver/Silver Chloride Electrode (Ag/AgCl):**

   - **Principle:** This electrode is based on the equilibrium between silver chloride and silver metal in the presence of chloride ions. It has a stable potential determined by the concentration of chloride ions in the electrolyte.
   - **Construction:** It comprises a silver wire coated with a layer of silver chloride, immersed in a potassium chloride solution.
   - **Advantages:** It is more practical for routine use due to its stability and ease of construction.

3. **Calomel Electrode (Mercury/Mercurous Chloride):**

   - **Principle:** This electrode works on the equilibrium between mercurous chloride and mercury metal in a chloride solution.
   - **Construction:** It includes a mercury pool covered with mercurous chloride, in contact with a saturated potassium chloride solution.

○ **Advantages:** Known for its stable and reproducible potential, making it popular in many analytical applications.

Criteria for an Ideal Reference Electrode:

- **Stable Potential:** The electrode should maintain a constant potential under various conditions.
- **Non-polarizable:** The potential should not change with the passage of current.
- **Reproducibility:** The potential should be reproducible across different measurements and setups.
- **Ease of Construction:** The electrode should be easy to assemble and maintain.

Applications in Pharmaceutical Analysis:

- **pH Measurements:** Reference electrodes are essential in pH meters to measure the hydrogen ion concentration in pharmaceutical solutions.
- **Titrations:** They are used in potentiometric titrations to detect the endpoint of the titration accurately.
- **Quality Control:** Reference electrodes help ensure the consistency and quality of pharmaceutical products by providing precise electrochemical measurements.

Maintenance and Calibration:

- Regular maintenance and calibration are crucial to ensure the accuracy and longevity of reference electrodes.
- **Maintenance:** Includes periodic cleaning, refilling of electrolyte solutions, and checking for any physical damage or contamination.
- **Calibration:** Ensures the electrode potential remains accurate. This is typically done using standard solutions with known potentials.

8.2.3 Indicator Electrodes

Introduction: Indicator electrodes, also known as sensing electrodes, are used in potentiometric measurements to indicate changes in the analyte concentration. These electrodes respond to specific ions in the solution, and their potential varies according to the ion activity. Indicator electrodes can be broadly categorized into metal electrodes and glass electrodes.

8.2.3.1 Metal Electrodes

Principle: Metal electrodes operate based on the redox reactions that occur at the metal surface when it comes into contact with the analyte solution. The potential of the metal electrode depends on the concentration of the analyte ions involved in the redox process.

Types and Examples:

- **Platinum Electrode:** Commonly used in redox titrations due to its inertness and wide potential range. It is suitable for detecting various ions like hydrogen, chlorine, and oxygen.
- **Silver Electrode:** Often used in conjunction with the silver/silver chloride reference electrode. It is particularly useful for detecting halide ions like chloride and bromide.
- **Copper Electrode:** Used for detecting copper ions and is employed in various complexometric titrations.
- **Gold Electrode:** Preferred in applications involving highly oxidative or corrosive environments due to its high resistance to corrosion.

Applications:

- **Redox Titrations:** Metal electrodes are extensively used in titrations involving oxidation-reduction reactions to determine the endpoint.
- **Ion-Selective Measurements:** Certain metal electrodes are selective to specific ions and are used in ion-selective potentiometry.
- **Pharmaceutical Analysis:** Used to determine the concentration of active pharmaceutical ingredients and trace metals in formulations.

Advantages and Disadvantages:

- **Advantages:** High sensitivity and selectivity for specific ions, robust, and versatile.
- **Disadvantages:** May suffer from interference by other ions, require frequent calibration, and can be expensive.

8.2.3.2 Glass Electrode

Principle: The glass electrode, primarily used for pH measurements, functions based on the exchange of hydrogen ions between the glass membrane and the solution. The potential difference across the glass membrane is directly proportional to the pH of the solution.

Construction:

- **Glass Membrane:** The key component is the thin glass membrane, which is selective to hydrogen ions.
- **Internal Solution:** Typically contains a known concentration of hydrogen ions (usually a buffered solution).
- **Internal Reference Electrode:** Often a silver/silver chloride electrode immersed in the internal solution.

Applications:

- **pH Measurement:** The glass electrode is the most common pH sensor in laboratories and industrial applications.
- **Quality Control:** Used in pharmaceutical industries to monitor the pH of solutions, ensuring they meet the required specifications.
- **Biochemical Applications:** Employed in biological research for monitoring pH in cell culture media and other biological fluids.

Advantages and Disadvantages:

- **Advantages:** High accuracy, wide pH range, and robust performance in various types of solutions.
- **Disadvantages:** Fragile, requires careful handling and regular calibration, and can be affected by high ionic strength and temperature variations.

8.2.4 End Point Determination Methods

Introduction: End point determination in potentiometric titrations is critical for accurate analytical results. It involves identifying the point at which the reaction between the analyte and the titrant is complete. Various methods can be employed to determine the end point in potentiometric titrations.

Methods:
1. Direct Method:

- **Description:** The potential of the indicator electrode is continuously measured and plotted against the volume of titrant added. The point where there is a sudden change in potential corresponds to the end point.
- **Advantages:** Simple and straightforward, does not require additional reagents or indicators.
- **Disadvantages:** Requires precise measurement and careful observation of the potential change.

2. First Derivative Method:

- **Description:** In this method, the first derivative of the potential with respect to the volume of titrant added is plotted. The peak in the first derivative curve corresponds to the end point.
- **Advantages:** More accurate than the direct method, especially for titrations with gradual potential changes.
- **Disadvantages:** Requires mathematical manipulation and data processing.

3. Second Derivative Method:

- **Description:** The second derivative of the potential with respect to the volume of titrant added is plotted. The point where the second derivative curve crosses zero indicates the end point.
- **Advantages:** Provides a clear and precise end point, especially useful for complex titrations.
- **Disadvantages:** Requires advanced data analysis techniques.

4. Gran Plot Method:

- **Description:** A Gran plot involves plotting the volume of titrant against a function of the potential. The linear portion of the plot is extrapolated to find the end point.
- **Advantages:** Effective for weak acid-weak base titrations and provides accurate results.

- **Disadvantages:** Requires careful plotting and interpretation of the data.

Applications in Pharmaceutical Analysis:
1. Quality Control: Accurate end point determination is crucial for ensuring the correct dosage of active pharmaceutical ingredients (APIs) in formulations. **2. Purity Testing:** Used to determine the purity of raw materials and final products by identifying impurities through titrations. **3. Stability Studies:** Helps in monitoring the stability of pharmaceutical products by assessing changes in their composition over time. **4. Assay of APIs:** Essential for quantifying the active ingredients in various dosage forms to ensure they meet the specified standards.

8.2.5 Applications in Pharmaceutical Analysis
Introduction: Potentiometry, particularly with the use of indicator electrodes, plays a pivotal role in pharmaceutical analysis. It is employed in various stages of drug development, quality control, and regulatory compliance to ensure the safety, efficacy, and quality of pharmaceutical products.

Applications:
1. pH Measurement:

- **Importance:** Accurate pH measurement is crucial in the formulation of pharmaceuticals, as it affects the stability, solubility, and bioavailability of drugs.
- **Example:** Determining the pH of injectable solutions to ensure they are within the acceptable range for patient safety.

2. Assay of Active Pharmaceutical Ingredients (APIs):

- **Importance:** Potentiometric titrations are used to determine the exact concentration of APIs in drug formulations.
- **Example:** Assaying the concentration of aspirin in tablets using potentiometric titration with a suitable indicator electrode.

3. Determination of Water Content:

- **Importance:** Monitoring water content is essential for the stability of hygroscopic drugs.

- **Example:** Karl Fischer titration, a type of potentiometric titration, is used to determine the water content in pharmaceuticals.

4. Analysis of Excipients:

- **Importance:** Excipients play a critical role in drug delivery and efficacy, and their concentration needs to be precisely controlled.
- **Example:** Potentiometric titration is used to determine the concentration of magnesium stearate in tablet formulations.

5. Stability Testing:

- **Importance:** Stability testing ensures that drugs maintain their efficacy and safety throughout their shelf life.
- **Example:** Monitoring the pH and other properties of a drug solution over time to assess its stability.

6. Dissolution Testing:

- **Importance:** Dissolution testing is essential for understanding the release profile of drugs from their dosage forms.
- **Example:** Using potentiometry to monitor the dissolution of a tablet in a simulated gastric fluid.

7. Detection of Impurities:

- **Importance:** Identifying and quantifying impurities is crucial for drug safety and regulatory compliance.
- **Example:** Potentiometric titration can detect trace levels of impurities such as heavy metals in pharmaceutical products.

8. Electrolyte Analysis:

- **Importance:** Electrolyte balance is vital for drug formulation and patient safety.
- **Example:** Determining the concentration of sodium and potassium ions in parenteral solutions using ion-selective electrodes.

Potentiometry, with its various techniques and applications, is an indispensable tool in pharmaceutical analysis. It provides accurate, reliable, and efficient means of ensuring the quality and safety of pharmaceutical products. Understanding the principles and applications of potentiometry allows for better control over the manufacturing process and compliance with regulatory standards.

CHAPTER IX

Polarography

9.1 Principles of Polarography

9.1.1 Introduction and Theory

Introduction: Polarography is an electrochemical analysis method that involves measuring the current that flows through a solution as a function of an applied voltage. This technique is particularly useful for analyzing trace amounts of metal ions and organic compounds. It was developed by Jaroslav Heyrovský, who received the Nobel Prize in Chemistry in 1959 for his invention.

Theory: Polarography operates on the principle of voltammetry, where the current resulting from the reduction or oxidation of analytes at an electrode is measured. The most common setup includes a dropping mercury electrode (DME) or a static mercury drop electrode (SMDE) as the working electrode, a reference electrode (such as a saturated calomel electrode), and a counter electrode.

Key Concepts:

1. Dropping Mercury Electrode (DME):

- **Description:** The DME continuously releases small drops of mercury into the solution, providing a constantly renewing surface that minimizes contamination and allows for high sensitivity.
- **Advantages:** High sensitivity and reproducibility, suitable for detecting trace elements.
- **Disadvantages:** Mercury toxicity requires careful handling and disposal.

2. Electrode Reactions:

- **Reduction:** Analytes gain electrons at the cathode (negative electrode), leading to a reduction reaction.
- **Oxidation:** Analytes lose electrons at the anode (positive electrode), leading to an oxidation reaction.

3. Polarogram:

- **Definition:** A plot of current (measured in microamperes) versus applied voltage (measured in millivolts).
- **Interpretation:** The peaks or waves in a polarogram correspond to specific electrochemical reactions of analytes. The position and height of these peaks provide qualitative and quantitative information about the analytes.

4. Electrolyte Solution:

- **Purpose:** An inert supporting electrolyte is used to carry the current and maintain a constant ionic strength, reducing the interference from other ions.
- **Example:** Sodium chloride or potassium nitrate solutions.

5. Current Components:

- **Faradaic Current:** Directly related to the redox reaction of the analyte.
- **Non-Faradaic Current:** Arises from the charging of the double layer at the electrode surface and does not contribute to the analytical signal.

Applications:

- **Trace Metal Analysis:** Detection of metals like lead, cadmium, and zinc in water, soil, and biological samples.
- **Organic Compounds:** Analysis of vitamins, antibiotics, and other organic molecules.
- **Environmental Monitoring:** Measurement of pollutants and contaminants in environmental samples.

Conclusion: Polarography is a powerful analytical tool in electrochemistry, offering high sensitivity and selectivity for various analytes. Understanding the fundamental principles and theory behind polarography is essential for its effective application in pharmaceutical analysis and other fields.

9.1.2 Ilkovic Equation

Introduction: The Ilkovic equation is fundamental to understanding the quantitative aspects of polarography. It relates the diffusion current in a polarographic experiment to the concentration of the analyte, the properties of the electrode, and the solution.

Ilkovic Equation:

$$Id = kn\, D^{1/2}\, m^{2/3}\, t^{1/6}\, C$$

Where:

- **I_d:** Diffusion current (measured in microamperes, µA)
- **k:** Constant (dependent on the units used for other variables)
- **n:** Number of electrons transferred in the redox reaction
- **D:** Diffusion coefficient of the analyte (cm^2/s)
- **m:** Rate of mercury drop formation (mg/s)
- **t:** Drop time (s)
- **C:** Concentration of the analyte (mol/L)

Explanation:
1. Diffusion Current (I_d):

- **Definition:** The current resulting from the reduction or oxidation of the analyte due to diffusion to the electrode surface.
- **Significance:** Directly proportional to the analyte concentration, allowing for quantitative analysis.

2. Number of Electrons (n):

- **Importance:** Indicates the number of electrons involved in the electrochemical reaction. It is crucial for determining the stoichiometry of the reaction.

3. Diffusion Coefficient (D):

- **Role:** Describes how quickly the analyte diffuses through the solution to the electrode surface. It depends on the size and nature of the analyte and the viscosity of the solution.

4. Mercury Drop Rate (m) and Drop Time (t):

- **Impact:** Influence the surface area of the dropping mercury electrode. The drop size and formation rate affect the sensitivity and resolution of the polarographic analysis.

Applications:

- **Quantitative Analysis:** Used to calculate the concentration of analytes in various samples by measuring the diffusion current.
- **Calibration:** Helps in calibrating the polarographic setup by establishing the relationship between current and concentration for known standards.
- **Electrochemical Studies:** Assists in understanding the kinetics and mechanisms of electrochemical reactions involving different analytes.

9.2 Electrodes in Polarography
9.2.1 Dropping Mercury Electrode (DME)

Introduction: The Dropping Mercury Electrode (DME) is a crucial component in polarographic analysis. It provides a continuously renewing surface, which is highly advantageous for achieving reproducible results and high sensitivity. Developed by Jaroslav Heyrovský, the DME's unique properties make it particularly suitable for studying reduction reactions and detecting trace amounts of various analytes.

Description and Construction: The DME consists of a fine capillary tube through which mercury flows and forms droplets at the tip. These droplets fall into the solution at a constant rate, creating a new, clean electrode surface with each drop. The apparatus typically includes:

- **Mercury Reservoir:** Holds the mercury that flows through the capillary.
- **Capillary Tube:** A fine tube that controls the flow rate of mercury.
- **Dropping Mechanism:** Ensures the formation and release of mercury drops at a consistent rate.

Advantages:

- **Renewing Surface:** The continuously renewing mercury surface minimizes contamination and adsorptive effects, leading to more accurate and reproducible results.
- **High Sensitivity:** The fresh mercury surface enhances the detection of trace levels of analytes.
- **Wide Potential Range:** Mercury has a large cathodic potential range, allowing the study of a variety of reduction processes.

Disadvantages:

- **Toxicity:** Mercury is highly toxic, requiring careful handling, proper ventilation, and disposal protocols to prevent environmental contamination and health hazards.
- **Limited Use:** Not suitable for analytes that form amalgams with mercury, which can alter the electrochemical properties of the electrode.

Operational Principles: During polarographic analysis, the potential applied to the DME is varied, and the resulting current is measured. The key factors influencing the performance of the DME include:

- **Drop Time:** The interval between the formation of consecutive drops. It affects the surface area and the diffusion layer.
- **Drop Size:** The volume of each mercury drop, which influences the current response.
- **Supporting Electrolyte:** An inert electrolyte added to the solution to ensure adequate conductivity and minimize migration effects.

Polarographic Waves: The current-voltage curve obtained during polarography is known as a polarogram. It typically features waves or peaks corresponding to the reduction or oxidation of analytes. The characteristics of these waves (such as half-wave potential and wave height) provide qualitative and quantitative information about the analyte.

Applications:

- **Trace Metal Analysis:** DME is extensively used for detecting and quantifying trace metals like lead, cadmium, and zinc in environmental and biological samples.

- **Organic Compound Analysis:** Suitable for analyzing organic compounds, including vitamins, antibiotics, and drugs.
- **Environmental Monitoring:** Effective in measuring pollutants and contaminants in water, soil, and air samples.

Example Studies:

1. **Lead Detection in Water:** A study used DME to measure lead concentration in drinking water. The polarogram showed a well-defined wave at a specific potential, indicating the presence of lead. By comparing the wave height to standard solutions, the lead concentration was determined to be within safe limits set by regulatory authorities.
2. **Vitamin Analysis:** Polarographic analysis of vitamin B1 in pharmaceutical preparations involved using DME. The technique provided accurate quantification of the vitamin content, ensuring compliance with quality standards.

Conclusion: The Dropping Mercury Electrode remains a pivotal tool in polarography, offering high sensitivity and reproducibility for a wide range of analytes. Despite its toxicity concerns, the DME's ability to provide a clean, renewable surface makes it indispensable in electrochemical analysis. Understanding its construction, advantages, and operational principles is essential for leveraging its full potential in scientific research and industrial applications.

9.3 Applications of Polarography

9.3.1 Pharmaceutical and Chemical Analysis

Introduction: Polarography, an electrochemical method based on the measurement of current as a function of applied voltage, has extensive applications in pharmaceutical and chemical analysis. This technique, with its high sensitivity and specificity, is particularly valuable for detecting and quantifying trace amounts of various substances. Its applications span from quality control in pharmaceutical manufacturing to environmental monitoring and biochemical research.

Pharmaceutical Analysis:

Drug Assay and Purity Testing: Polarography is frequently used to determine the concentration of active pharmaceutical ingredients (APIs) in drugs. For example, the content of antibiotics, vitamins, and hormones in formulations can be accurately measured using polarographic techniques. This ensures that the drugs meet the required standards for efficacy and safety.

Detection of Impurities: Impurities in pharmaceuticals, even at trace levels, can affect the drug's safety and efficacy. Polarography is highly effective in detecting and quantifying these impurities. For instance, heavy metal contaminants like lead, cadmium, and mercury, which can be harmful even in small amounts, can be identified in pharmaceutical products.

Stability Studies: The stability of pharmaceuticals under various conditions is crucial for determining their shelf life and storage requirements. Polarographic analysis can monitor the degradation products of drugs over time, providing valuable data for stability studies. This helps in establishing the appropriate storage conditions and expiry dates for pharmaceutical products.

Chemical Analysis:

Trace Metal Analysis: Polarography is widely used for the detection and quantification of trace metals in various samples. In environmental analysis, it can measure metals like zinc, copper, and nickel in water and soil samples, helping in pollution monitoring and control. In the food industry, it ensures that metal contaminants in food products are within safe limits.

Organic Compound Analysis: Organic compounds such as phenols, amines, and antioxidants can be analyzed using polarography. This is particularly useful in studying the electrochemical behavior of these compounds and understanding their redox properties. Such analyses are essential in fields like organic synthesis, environmental chemistry, and materials science.

Biochemical Applications: In biochemical research, polarography can analyze biomolecules such as enzymes, nucleotides, and vitamins. It is used to study the redox behavior of these molecules and their interactions with other compounds. This aids in understanding biochemical pathways and developing new therapeutic agents.

9.3.2 Case Studies and Examples

Case Study 1: Detection of Lead in Drinking Water A study aimed to measure the concentration of lead in drinking water samples using polarography. The water samples were collected from various sources, and the analysis revealed the presence of lead at different concentrations. The polarogram displayed characteristic peaks for lead, allowing for precise quantification. The study concluded that some water sources had lead levels exceeding the safety limits set by regulatory authorities, prompting further investigation and remedial action.

Case Study 2: Assay of Vitamin B1 in Pharmaceutical Preparations Polarographic analysis was employed to determine the content of vitamin B1 (thiamine) in various pharmaceutical formulations. The samples were prepared and subjected to polarographic analysis, which produced distinct waves corresponding to the reduction of thiamine. By comparing the wave heights with standard solutions, the vitamin B1 content in each formulation was accurately quantified. This ensured that the products complied with quality standards, guaranteeing their therapeutic efficacy.

Example 1: Analysis of Heavy Metals in Food Products Polarography was used to analyze heavy metal contaminants in canned food products. The study aimed to ensure that the levels of metals such as cadmium and mercury were within permissible limits. The polarographic analysis detected the presence of these metals, and the results were compared to regulatory standards. The study confirmed that the food products were safe for consumption, highlighting the importance of regular monitoring for food safety.

Example 2: Stability Testing of Antioxidants in Cosmetics A cosmetic product containing antioxidants was subjected to polarographic analysis to monitor the stability of the antioxidants over time. The study involved storing the product under different conditions and analyzing it at regular intervals. The polarograms showed changes in the antioxidant content, indicating the degradation of the active ingredients. This data was used to optimize the formulation and storage conditions, ensuring the product's efficacy and shelf life.

Polarography is a versatile and powerful technique with broad applications in pharmaceutical and chemical analysis. Its ability to detect and quantify trace amounts of substances makes it indispensable in quality control, environmental monitoring, and research. By providing accurate and reliable data, polarography plays a crucial role in ensuring the safety, efficacy, and quality of various products and materials.

CHAPTER X

Gravimetric Analysis

10.1.1 Introduction to Gravimetric Analysis

Introduction to Gravimetric Analysis

Gravimetric analysis is a core method in analytical chemistry where the mass of a substance is used to determine its quantity or concentration. This technique relies on measuring the weight of a pure compound that contains the analyte. Gravimetric analysis stands out due to its high accuracy and precision, making it an essential tool in both research and industry. It involves a series of well-defined steps, including precipitation, filtration, washing, drying or igniting, and weighing the analyte. The method is highly valued because it provides results with minimal errors when carefully performed.

Gravimetric analysis begins with the conversion of the analyte into a pure, stable compound that can be isolated and weighed. This process typically involves forming a precipitate through a chemical reaction, which is then separated from the solution. The precipitate is washed to remove impurities, dried or ignited to a constant weight, and finally weighed. The weight of the precipitate is used to calculate the quantity of the analyte based on its known chemical composition.

Basic Principles

The basic principles of gravimetric analysis involve several critical steps:

Precipitation: The first step in gravimetric analysis is to convert the analyte into a solid precipitate. This is achieved by adding a reagent that reacts with the analyte to form an insoluble compound. The choice of precipitating reagent is crucial, as it must produce a pure, easily filterable precipitate.

Filtration: After precipitation, the solid must be separated from the liquid. Filtration techniques are used to collect the precipitate on a filter medium, such as filter paper or a sintered glass crucible. The goal is to ensure that all of the precipitate is collected without loss.

Washing of Precipitate: The precipitate is washed to remove any adhering impurities, such as soluble salts or by-products. Washing must be thorough but careful to avoid loss of the precipitate. The washing liquid is typically a dilute solution of the precipitating reagent to prevent dissolution of the precipitate.

Drying or Igniting Precipitate: The washed precipitate is then dried or ignited to remove any remaining moisture or volatile components. Drying is performed at a relatively low temperature, while ignition involves heating to a higher temperature to decompose or volatilize impurities.

Weighing the Precipitate: The final step is to accurately weigh the dried or ignited precipitate. The weight of the precipitate is used to calculate the quantity of the analyte based on the stoichiometry of the chemical reaction used to form the precipitate.

Analytical Balance

An analytical balance is a crucial instrument in gravimetric analysis. It provides the precise measurements required to ensure accuracy. Modern analytical balances are capable of measuring to the nearest microgram, allowing for extremely precise quantification of the analyte. Proper calibration and handling of the balance are essential to maintain accuracy.

Types of Precipitates

Precipitates in gravimetric analysis can be classified into two main types: crystalline and amorphous.

Crystalline Precipitates: These are precipitates with a well-defined crystal structure. They tend to be more easily filtered and washed, making them ideal for gravimetric analysis. Examples include barium sulfate and silver chloride.

Amorphous Precipitates: These lack a defined crystal structure and are often more gelatinous and difficult to filter. They require careful handling to avoid losses. Examples include ferric hydroxide and aluminum hydroxide.

Factors Affecting Precipitation

Several factors can influence the formation and quality of precipitates in gravimetric analysis:

Temperature: Higher temperatures can increase the solubility of the precipitate, reducing the yield. Conversely, lower temperatures may enhance precipitation but can also lead to the formation of fine particles that are difficult to filter.

pH of the Solution: The pH can significantly affect the solubility of the precipitate. Many precipitates are more soluble in acidic or basic conditions, so controlling the pH is essential for optimal precipitation.

Concentration of Reactants: The concentrations of the analyte and the precipitating reagent must be carefully controlled. Too high a concentration can lead to rapid precipitation and the formation of impure precipitates, while too low a concentration may result in incomplete precipitation.

Co-precipitation and Post-precipitation

In gravimetric analysis, it is crucial to understand and minimize the effects of co-precipitation and post-precipitation.

Co-precipitation: This occurs when impurities precipitate along with the desired analyte, leading to inaccurate results. Co-precipitation can happen through various mechanisms, including surface adsorption, mixed crystal formation, occlusion, and mechanical entrapment. Techniques such as digestion (allowing the precipitate to stand in the mother liquor) can help reduce co-precipitation.

Post-precipitation: This occurs when impurities precipitate after the desired analyte has formed and been filtered. This can be minimized by carefully controlling the precipitation conditions and ensuring thorough washing of the precipitate.

Applications of Gravimetric Analysis

Gravimetric analysis is widely used in various fields due to its high accuracy and precision. In pharmaceuticals, it is used for quality control and purity testing of raw materials and finished products. In environmental analysis, it is employed to determine the concentration of pollutants in air and water. In the food industry, gravimetric methods are used to analyze the composition of food products.

Estimation of Barium Sulfate

The estimation of barium sulfate serves as a classic example of gravimetric analysis. Barium ions are precipitated as barium sulfate by adding sulfuric acid. The precipitate is filtered, washed, dried or ignited, and weighed. The mass of barium sulfate is then used to calculate the concentration of barium in the original sample.

Procedure for Estimation

The procedure involves several key steps:

1. **Preparation of Sample**: The sample solution containing barium ions is prepared.

2. **Addition of Sulfate Reagent**: A sulfuric acid solution is added to precipitate barium sulfate.

3. **Formation of Barium Sulfate Precipitate**: The precipitate is allowed to form and settle.
4. **Filtration and Washing of Precipitate**: The precipitate is filtered and washed to remove impurities.
5. **Drying or Igniting the Precipitate**: The washed precipitate is dried or ignited to a constant weight.
6. **Weighing the Precipitate**: The final weight of the precipitate is measured.

Calculations Involved

The calculations involve determining the molar mass of barium sulfate and using the stoichiometry of the reaction to find the concentration of barium in the original sample. The percentage yield and purity of the sample can also be calculated based on the weight of the precipitate.

Conclusion

Gravimetric analysis remains a fundamental technique in analytical chemistry due to its high precision and accuracy. By understanding and carefully controlling the various steps and factors involved, accurate and reliable results can be obtained. Whether for quality control in pharmaceuticals or environmental analysis, gravimetric methods continue to be an essential part of the analytical chemist's toolkit.

This expanded introduction to gravimetric analysis provides a comprehensive overview, ensuring a deep understanding of the principles and practices involved.

10.1.2 Basic Principles

10.1.2.1 Precipitation

Precipitation is the foundational step in gravimetric analysis. It involves converting the analyte into an insoluble solid, known as a precipitate, through a chemical reaction. The reagent used must react specifically and completely with the analyte to form a pure precipitate. The reaction conditions, such as concentration, temperature, and pH, must be carefully controlled to ensure the formation of a precipitate that is pure, dense, and easily filterable. Common precipitants include silver nitrate for chloride, sulfuric acid for barium, and oxalic acid for calcium.

The process of precipitation can be described by the reaction:

$$Ba^{2+} + SO_4^{2-} \rightarrow BaSO_4$$

In this reaction, barium ions to form barium sulfate, an insoluble precipitate. The quality of the precipitate is crucial as it determines the accuracy and precision of the analysis. Ideally, the precipitate should form slowly to allow the formation of large, easily filterable crystals. Rapid precipitation can lead to the formation of fine, colloidal particles that are difficult to filter and wash, leading to potential errors in the final measurement.

10.1.2.2 Filtration

Filtration is the process of separating the solid precipitate from the liquid phase, known as the supernatant. This step is critical to ensure that all of the precipitate is collected for subsequent analysis. Filtration methods include using filter paper, sintered glass crucibles, or vacuum filtration setups, depending on the nature and quantity of the precipitate. The goal is to achieve complete separation with minimal loss of the precipitate.

The choice of filtration medium depends on the characteristics of the precipitate. For instance, coarse precipitates can be filtered using standard filter paper, while fine precipitates might require a more porous medium, such as a sintered glass crucible. The filtration setup must be properly calibrated to ensure efficient separation without clogging or loss of material.

10.1.2.3 Washing of Precipitate

Washing the precipitate is essential to remove any impurities that may be co-precipitated or adsorbed on the surface of the precipitate. These impurities can include soluble salts, unreacted reagents, or other contaminants. The washing process must be thorough yet gentle to prevent the loss of the precipitate.

Typically, the washing liquid is a dilute solution of the precipitating reagent or a volatile solvent like ethanol. This helps in minimizing the solubility of the precipitate during washing. The process involves adding small amounts of the washing liquid to the precipitate, allowing it to percolate through, and then discarding the washings. This step is repeated several times until the precipitate is free of impurities.

10.1.2.4 Drying or Igniting Precipitate

After washing, the precipitate must be dried or ignited to remove any remaining moisture or volatile substances. Drying is usually done at a temperature that ensures complete removal of water without decomposing the precipitate. In some cases, the precipitate needs to be ignited, which involves heating it to a high temperature to remove any remaining volatile components and convert the precipitate into a stable, anhydrous form.

The drying or ignition process can be represented as:

$$CaC_2O_4 \cdot H2O \rightarrow CaC_2O_4 + H2O$$

In this reaction, calcium oxalate monohydrate is heated to remove water, resulting in anhydrous calcium oxalate

The choice between drying and ignition depends on the nature of the precipitate and the required accuracy of the analysis. Drying is usually sufficient for most precipitates, while ignition is necessary for those that contain volatile impurities or need to be converted to a stable form.

10.1.2.5 Weighing the Precipitate

Weighing the precipitate is the final and most critical step in gravimetric analysis. The accuracy of the analysis depends on precise and accurate measurement of the precipitate's mass. An analytical balance, capable of measuring to the nearest microgram, is typically used for this purpose.

The weighing process must be conducted under controlled conditions to avoid errors due to moisture absorption, static electricity, or air currents. The precipitate is transferred to a pre-weighed container, and its mass is measured. The weight of the container with the precipitate is then compared to the initial weight of the empty container to determine the mass of the precipitate.

The calculated mass of the precipitate is used to determine the concentration of the analyte in the original sample based on the stoichiometry of the reaction. For example, in the estimation of sulfate as barium sulfate:

$$SO4^{2-} + Ba^{2+} \rightarrow BaSO_4$$

The mass of $BaSO_4$ is used to calculate the amount of $SO4^{2-}$ in the sample. The results are reported with appropriate units and precision, reflecting the accuracy of the gravimetric analysis.

In conclusion, gravimetric analysis is a precise and accurate method of quantitative chemical analysis. By understanding and controlling each step in the process—precipitation, filtration, washing, drying or igniting, and weighing—the analyst can obtain reliable results. This method is widely used in various fields, including pharmaceuticals, environmental analysis, and materials science, due to its robustness and reliability.

10.1.3 Analytical Balance

An **analytical balance** is a critical instrument in gravimetric analysis. It is designed to measure small masses with high precision and accuracy, often to the nearest microgram (0.000001 grams). The analytical balance consists of a weighing pan enclosed in a draft shield to prevent air currents from affecting the measurement.

Key features of an analytical balance include:

- **Precision**: High-resolution measurement capability, typically to four or five decimal places.
- **Calibration**: Regular calibration with standard weights to maintain accuracy.
- **Stability**: A stable platform to minimize vibrations and disturbances.
- **Temperature Control**: Ensuring the balance operates within a specified temperature range to prevent measurement errors due to thermal expansion or contraction.

The weighing process involves placing the sample in a pre-weighed container or crucible, allowing the balance to stabilize, and recording the mass. The accuracy of this step is crucial as it directly affects the reliability of the final analytical results. Proper handling and maintenance of the analytical balance are essential to achieve consistent and accurate measurements.

10.1.4 Types of Precipitates

10.1.4.1 Crystalline Precipitates

Crystalline precipitates are characterized by their well-defined geometric shapes and orderly internal structures. These precipitates form when the conditions favor slow and controlled crystal growth, allowing the ions to arrange themselves into a stable lattice structure. Crystalline precipitates are typically easier to filter and wash due to their larger particle size and lower tendency to trap impurities.

Examples include:

- **Barium sulfate ($BaSO_4$)**: Formed by the reaction of barium ions with sulfate ions.
- **Calcium oxalate (CaC_2O_4)**: Precipitated from a solution containing calcium and oxalate ions.

The formation of crystalline precipitates can be influenced by factors such as temperature, concentration, and the rate of reagent addition. Slow addition of reagents and maintaining a low supersaturation level help in forming large, well-defined crystals.

10.1.4.2 Amorphous Precipitates

Amorphous precipitates lack a defined crystal structure and are generally formed by rapid precipitation, leading to the formation of fine, colloidal particles. These precipitates can be more challenging to filter and wash due to their tendency to form gelatinous masses that trap impurities and solvent molecules.

Examples include:

- **Ferric hydroxide (Fe(OH)$_3$):** Precipitated from solutions containing ferric ions and hydroxide ions.
- **Aluminum hydroxide (Al(OH)$_3$):** Formed by the reaction of aluminum ions with hydroxide ions.

Amorphous precipitates are often formed under conditions of high supersaturation, where the rapid nucleation rate outpaces the growth rate of individual particles. Controlling the precipitation conditions, such as by using slow addition of reagents and maintaining a lower concentration of reactants, can help mitigate the formation of amorphous precipitates.

10.1.5 Factors Affecting Precipitation

10.1.5.1 Temperature

Temperature plays a significant role in the precipitation process. Higher temperatures generally increase the solubility of most salts, reducing the tendency for precipitation. Conversely, lower temperatures decrease solubility, promoting precipitation. However, the temperature must be controlled carefully as excessive cooling can lead to the formation of fine, colloidal particles instead of the desired crystalline form.

For example, the solubility of barium sulfate decreases significantly with a drop in temperature, leading to more efficient precipitation at lower temperatures. Maintaining an optimal temperature range is crucial for achieving the desired precipitate characteristics.

10.1.5.2 pH of the Solution

The **pH of the solution** is another critical factor that affects precipitation. The solubility of many precipitates is pH-dependent, with certain precipitates forming only within specific pH ranges. Adjusting the pH can help in selectively precipitating specific ions while keeping others in solution.

For instance, ferric hydroxide precipitates readily in basic conditions but remains soluble in acidic solutions. By controlling the pH, it is possible to achieve selective precipitation of target analytes. The pH can be adjusted using suitable buffers or by adding acids or bases to the solution.

10.1.5.3 Concentration of Reactants

The **concentration of reactants** influences the rate and completeness of precipitation. High concentrations of the reactants can lead to rapid nucleation and formation of fine, amorphous precipitates. On the other hand, lower concentrations and slow addition of reagents promote the growth of larger, crystalline precipitates.

The principle of supersaturation is key to understanding this effect. Supersaturation occurs when the concentration of ions exceeds their equilibrium solubility. Controlling the rate of reagent addition helps manage the level of supersaturation, thus affecting the nature of the precipitate formed.

By carefully controlling these factors—temperature, pH, and concentration of reactants—analysts can optimize the precipitation process to produce pure, easily filterable precipitates suitable for gravimetric analysis. This control ensures the accuracy and reliability of the analytical results, making gravimetric analysis a robust method for quantitative chemical analysis.

10.2 Co-precipitation and Post-precipitation

10.2.1 Definition and Mechanisms

10.2.1.1 Co-precipitation

Co-precipitation is a process where impurities are incorporated into a precipitate during its formation. These impurities can be adsorbed on the surface, trapped within the crystal lattice, or physically occluded within the precipitate. This phenomenon occurs even when the impurities are present in trace amounts and can significantly affect the purity and mass of the final precipitate, leading to errors in gravimetric analysis.

Mechanisms of co-precipitation include:

- **Surface Adsorption**: Impurities adhere to the surface of the growing crystals.
- **Mixed Crystals Formation**: Impurities replace some of the ions in the crystal lattice.
- **Occlusion**: Impurities are trapped within the growing crystals.
- **Mechanical Entrapment**: Impurities are physically trapped within the precipitate mass.

10.2.1.2 Post-precipitation

Post-precipitation occurs when impurities precipitate onto the surface of a previously formed precipitate after the initial precipitation process is complete. This can happen due to changes in the solution's conditions, such as pH, temperature, or concentration of reactants, leading to the precipitation of additional, unwanted substances.

Mechanisms of post-precipitation include:

- **Secondary Precipitation**: Formation of new precipitates on the surface of the original precipitate.
- **Surface Adsorption**: Adsorption of impurities onto the surface of the existing precipitate.

10.2.2 Types of Co-precipitation
10.2.2.1 Surface Adsorption

Surface adsorption occurs when impurity ions are adsorbed onto the surface of the precipitate during its formation. This is common when the precipitate has a large surface area or when the impurity ions have a strong affinity for the precipitate surface. Surface adsorption can be minimized by thorough washing of the precipitate with a suitable solvent to remove the adsorbed impurities.

10.2.2.2 Mixed Crystals Formation

Mixed crystals formation happens when impurity ions replace some of the ions in the crystal lattice of the precipitate. This is more likely to occur when the impurity ions have similar sizes and charges to the ions in the precipitate. Mixed crystals formation can be minimized by controlling the concentration of impurities and the conditions of precipitation, such as temperature and pH.

10.2.2.3 Occlusion

Occlusion occurs when impurities are trapped within the growing crystals of the precipitate. This can happen when the crystals form rapidly, trapping solution and impurities within the lattice. Occlusion can be minimized by allowing the precipitate to form slowly, giving the impurities time to diffuse out of the

10.3 Estimation Techniques

10.3.1 General Overview

Estimation techniques in gravimetric analysis involve several steps, including the formation of a precipitate, its separation from the solution, and accurate weighing to determine the amount of analyte. These techniques are crucial for obtaining precise and accurate results. The following sections will delve into various methods of precipitation, filtering, drying, and ignition, providing a comprehensive understanding of the processes involved.

10.3.2 Precipitation Methods

10.3.2.1 Precipitation from Homogeneous Solution

Precipitation from a homogeneous solution involves the formation of the precipitate within the solution itself, rather than by adding a precipitating agent. This method ensures uniform particle size and reduces the chances of co-precipitation. One common approach is to use a reagent that slowly decomposes to release the precipitating ion. For instance, urea can be used to gradually increase the pH of a solution, leading to the precipitation of metal hydroxides. This method offers advantages such as better control over the precipitation process and improved purity of the precipitate.

10.3.2.2 Direct Precipitation

Direct precipitation occurs when a precipitating agent is directly added to the solution containing the analyte. The choice of precipitating agent and the conditions of the reaction are critical for the successful formation of a pure precipitate. For example, silver nitrate can be added to a solution of chloride ions to form silver chloride precipitate. Control over factors such as temperature, pH, and concentration of reagents is essential to ensure complete and selective precipitation.

10.3.2.3 Indirect Precipitation

Indirect precipitation involves the conversion of the analyte into a different form that can then be precipitated. This technique is useful when the direct precipitation of the analyte is not feasible or practical. For example, phosphate ions can be precipitated indirectly by first converting them into a calcium phosphate compound, which can then be precipitated by adding a calcium salt. Indirect precipitation often requires additional steps and reagents, but it can provide more accurate and specific results.

10.3.3 Filtering Techniques

10.3.3.1 Filtration

Filtration is a common method for separating the precipitate from the solution. The precipitate is collected on a filter medium, such as filter paper, which allows the liquid to pass through while retaining the solid particles. The choice of filter medium depends on the size of the precipitate particles and the nature of the solution. Filtration is a straightforward and effective method, but it may not be suitable for very fine or colloidal precipitates.

10.3.3.2 Vacuum Filtration

Vacuum filtration is a more efficient method for separating the precipitate from the solution, especially for fine or colloidal precipitates. In this technique, a vacuum is applied to the filtration apparatus to speed up the process and improve the recovery of the precipitate. The precipitate is collected on a filter medium placed in a Buchner funnel, and the vacuum helps to pull the liquid through the filter, leaving the solid behind. Vacuum filtration is faster and more effective than simple filtration, but it requires specialized equipment.

10.3.3.3 Centrifugation

Centrifugation is used to separate precipitates that are difficult to filter. In this method, the solution containing the precipitate is placed in a centrifuge tube and spun at high speeds. The centrifugal force causes the precipitate to settle at the bottom of the tube, allowing the clear supernatant to be decanted. Centrifugation is particularly useful for very fine or colloidal precipitates and can achieve better separation than filtration. However, it requires access to a centrifuge and may involve additional steps to recover the precipitate.

10.3.4 Drying and Ignition Methods

10.3.4.1 Air Drying

Air drying involves leaving the precipitate in an open environment to allow the solvent to evaporate naturally. This method is simple and does not require specialized equipment, but it can be slow and may not remove all the moisture from the precipitate. Air drying is suitable for precipitates that are stable at room temperature and do not require high precision in the moisture content.

10.3.4.2 Oven Drying

Oven drying involves placing the precipitate in an oven set at a specific temperature to evaporate the solvent more quickly and thoroughly. The temperature and duration of drying depend on the nature of the precipitate and the solvent. Oven drying is faster and more efficient than air drying and can achieve a more consistent moisture content. However, it requires access to an oven and careful control of the drying conditions to avoid decomposition or loss of the precipitate.

10.3.4.3 Ignition

Ignition involves heating the precipitate to a high temperature to drive off all the volatile components, including moisture and any remaining solvent. This method is used when a completely dry and stable final product is required. The precipitate is placed in a crucible and heated in a muffle furnace to a temperature that ensures complete removal of volatile components without decomposing the analyte. Ignition provides a very accurate and stable final product but requires specialized equipment and careful control of the heating conditions.

By understanding these estimation techniques and their applications, one can achieve precise and accurate results in gravimetric analysis. Each method has its advantages and limitations, and the choice of technique depends on the specific requirements of the analysis.

10.4 Estimation of Barium Sulphate

10.4.1 Procedure for Estimation

10.4.1.1 Preparation of Sample

Preparation of the sample is the initial step in the estimation of barium sulphate. This involves accurately weighing a known quantity of the sample, which contains the barium ions to be precipitated. The sample is dissolved in an appropriate solvent, usually distilled water or a dilute acid, to ensure that the barium ions are fully in solution and ready for the precipitation reaction.

10.4.1.2 Addition of Sulfate Reagent

Addition of the sulfate reagent involves carefully introducing a reagent that contains sulfate ions to the barium ion solution. The most common sulfate reagent used is sulfuric acid or a soluble sulfate salt like sodium sulfate. The addition is typically done slowly and with constant stirring to ensure even distribution and to promote the formation of a fine precipitate.

10.4.1.3 Formation of Barium Sulphate Precipitate

Formation of barium sulphate precipitate occurs when barium ions react with sulfate ions to form barium sulfate ($BaSO_4$), which is insoluble in water. The chemical reaction is represented by the equation:

$$Ba^{2+} (aq) + SO4^{2-} (aq) \rightarrow BaSO_4 (s)$$

The formation of a fine, white precipitate indicates that the reaction is proceeding correctly. It is crucial to maintain the correct temperature and pH to ensure complete precipitation and to avoid co-precipitation of other ions.

10.4.1.4 Filtration and Washing of Precipitate

Filtration and washing of the precipitate involve separating the barium sulfate precipitate from the solution using a suitable filtration method, such as vacuum filtration or centrifugation. The precipitate is collected on a filter medium, usually filter paper. After filtration, the precipitate is washed several times with distilled water to remove any adhering impurities and soluble contaminants.

10.4.1.5 Drying or Igniting the Precipitate

Drying or igniting the precipitate is the next step, where the washed precipitate is dried in an oven at a controlled temperature to remove all moisture. Alternatively, the precipitate can be ignited in a muffle furnace to convert it to a stable, anhydrous form. The drying or ignition process ensures that the precipitate is in a consistent and weighable form.

10.4.1.6 Weighing the Precipitate

Weighing the precipitate is the final step in the estimation procedure. The dried or ignited barium sulfate precipitate is accurately weighed using an analytical balance. The mass of the precipitate is used to calculate the amount of barium present in the original sample, based on the stoichiometry of the precipitation reaction.

10.4.2 Calculations Involved

10.4.2.1 Calculation of Molar Mass

Calculation of molar mass involves determining the molar mass of barium sulfate ($BaSO_4$), which is calculated as follows:

Molar mass of BaSO4 = Ba(137.33 g/mol) + S(32.06 g/mol) + 4×O(16.00 g/mol) = 137.33 + 32.06 + 64.00 = 233.39 g/mol

This molar mass is used to convert the mass of the barium sulfate precipitate to moles.

10.4.2.2 Determination of Purity

Determination of purity involves calculating the percentage purity of barium in the sample based on the mass of the barium sulfate precipitate. The moles of barium are calculated from the mass of the precipitate, and the purity is determined as follows:

Moles of BaSO$_4$=Mass of BaSO$_4$ / Molar mass of BaSO$_4$

Purity(%)=(Moles of Ba in sample / Theoretical moles of Ba)×100

10.4.2.3 Percentage Yield

Percentage yield is calculated to determine the efficiency of the precipitation process. It is the ratio of the actual mass of the precipitate obtained to the theoretical mass of the precipitate expected, expressed as a percentage:

Percentage yield=(Actual mass of BaSO$_4$ / Theoretical mass of BaSO4)×100

10.4.3 Applications in Pharmaceutical Analysis

10.4.3.1 Quality Control

Quality control involves using gravimetric analysis to ensure the purity and correct composition of pharmaceutical substances. Barium sulfate estimation is particularly relevant in verifying the sulfate content in drugs and other formulations.

10.4.3.2 Purity Testing

Purity testing is essential to ensure that pharmaceutical products meet the required standards. Estimating barium sulfate helps in identifying and quantifying impurities that may affect the efficacy and safety of the drug.

10.4.3.3 Standardization

Standardization involves using gravimetric analysis to calibrate and validate other analytical methods. The precise determination of barium sulfate content helps in developing accurate standard operating procedures and ensuring consistency in pharmaceutical analysis.

CHAPTER XI

About Authors

Dr. LAGU SURENDRA BABU M.Pharm, Ph.D. Assistant Professor, Pharmaceutical Chemistry Division in Adikavi Nannaya University College of Pharmaceutical Sciences, AKNU-TPG campus, Tadepalligudem, W.G district, Andhra Pradesh, India. Doctor of Philosophy & Post Graduate from Andhra University College of Pharmaceutical Sciences, he ranked State third in AURCET-2017 Conducted by A. U and also qualified GPAT & NIPER. Graduate from Acharya Nagarjuna University College of Pharmaceutical Sciences. Total 08.5 experience in teaching, industry and Central Drugs Standard Control Organization (CDSCO).

His expertise in Development of analytical profiles for drugs by Chromatographic and Spectroscopic methods. Chemical Studies on Bioactive metabolites from medicinal plants. Design, planning & Development of Synthetic routes for the modification of bioactive natural products. Synthesis and evaluation of bioactive heterocyclic compounds by bioinformatics tools for screening potential Antimicrobial, Anti-tubercular and Anticancer, CNS activities. Effective team player with multi-tasking & analytical abilities. He has more than 30 publications in national and an international scientific journal, 01 book chapter, 02 books, 06 patents on his credits. He is a life time membership in InSc and APTI.

Motivating and endowed Pharmaceutical Sciences faculty with 08+ years of experience in teaching, mentoring, advising, curriculum design, people management, supporting and impacting the students to deliver the best professional performance. Constantly engaged in coaching and training the students by using interactive discussions, Power Point Presentations and Hands-on approach to help them learn the theoretical concepts of Pharmaceutical Analysis, Pharmaceutical Chemistry, Medicinal Chemistry and allied subjects and apply them in laboratory settings

Dr. SARAKULA PRASANTHI M.Sc., Ph.D, completed her PhD from one of the Prestigious University in India, Andhra University at the Department of Organic Chemistry & FDW under the supervision of Prof. V. Siddaiah. She was Awarded with the Meritorious UGC-RGNF Fellowship in her Research Period. She ranked State First in AURCET-2010 Conducted by Andhra University and also qualified APSET. She obtained her M.Sc. degree in Organic Chemistry Specialization from Andhra University and B. Sc in Chemistry from Pondicherry Central University. She worked as Assistant

Professor for 10 years in various UG & PG Colleges in AU and JNTUK. Till Date she has published 12 research papers in reputed international journals and also have one granted national patents and one granted international patent to her name. Her research expertise includes the synthesis of natural Products and biologically active molecules. She has been instrumental in the operation and analysis in various analytical tools for characterizing organic molecules like NMR, GC and HPLC. Since December 2021, she is serving as Assistant Professor in Department Of Chemistry at Adikavi Nannaya University, Tadepalligudem campus.

Dr. NAMMI USHA RANI M. Pharm, Ph.D. currently works as Professor at Maharajah's College of Pharmacy, Andhra Pradesh, India. She had her graduation, masters and doctorate from Andhra University, India. Her key areas of research are Spectroscopy and Chromatography holding vidvan ID 452889. She has been handling Pharmaceutical Analysis, Advanced Instrumental Techniques and Pharmaceutical Validation subjects for graduates and post graduates since past 20 years. She can be found on http://www.youtube.com/@dr.n.usharani7337 where her videos provide.

information on working principles and instrumentation of various analytical techniques